COLLABORATIVE CREATIVITY

COLLABORATIVE CREATIVITY
UNLEASHING THE POWER OF SHARED THINKING

Jack Ricchiuto

Oakhill Press
Akron & New York

Collaborative Creativity

Library of Congress Cataloging-in-Publication Data

Ricchiuto, Jack, 1952-
    Collaborative Creativity ; unleashing the power of shared thinking / Jack Ricchiuto.
    p.   cm.
    Includes bibliographical references.
    ISBN 1-886939-12-8
    1. Creative ability in business. 2. Cooperation I. Title.
HD53.R527   1996
658.4'036--dc20   96-43757
                                      CIP

0 9 8 7 6 5 4 3 2 1

First Printing, October 1996

Acknowledgments

This book was inspired in a thousand ways. My work with organizations over the past two decades, hundreds of conversations about collaboration and creativity with experts and practitioners, not to mention the growing body of research on creativity and innovation. Going further back from this, I am deeply grateful to my family for a sense of humor and community, my teachers for a sense of resourcefulness, and my creative friends for a sense of connection to the infinite field of possibilities.

Special acknowledgment goes to my wife, Cis, for her unconditional support and inspiration as an artist and teacher. Thanks to Roger Herman for encouragement to do this book, to Karl Ziellenbach and Joyce Gioia for their expert guidance and management of the project. Appreciation goes to Steve Augustine for his willingness to collaborate on the cover art and design.

Deepest appreciation goes to the organizations who invite me to speak, train, and consult on teamwork and innovation. These provide me with learning opportunities that are vital to my own development as expert in organizational development and creativity.

CONTENTS

Creating Together

Practicing Creativity

Designing Meetings

Winning Support

Creative Organizations

Preface

Collaborative Creativity is the confluence of richly diverse ideas, questions, and experiences. It brings together the "technology" of creativity as a discipline in itself, recent research and business applications from quantum physics and the natural sciences, examples of innovation in business and organizational development, some Buddhist enlightenment, and the inspiration of artists and inventors.

This book grew out of a need to give my clients a peek into the possibilities of creativity in their work. It is designed to take them to new levels of understanding and performance. It features memorable quotes from the best minds in the fields of creativity, innovation, and organizational development today. It provides exercises for the development of creative potentials, and encouragement to be as collaborative as possible in the creative process. A special feature is an introduction to a tool I have developed in my work with clients called the *Idea Garden* (page 78). It provides them with an interesting and powerful alternative to traditional "brainstorming."

It has become clear to many of us in the field of organizational development that, no matter what business you're in and no matter what your mission and vision, your organization will only succeed to the degree that it can build and sustain a vibrant culture of collaboration and creativity. Old ideas and individual efforts no longer cut the mustard. The most important opportunities and rewards will go to those who are inventive and boundaryless.

For organizations who are relying on unparalleled development of leadership, project, and work teams, you may have discovered that it is not enough just to put teams of people together, give them an objective, and let them run with it. Running often doesn't occur if people have not developed the competencies required for collaborative and creative thinking.

For people who have begun their education and apprenticeship in collaboration and creativity through other books and seminars, *Collaborative Creativity* provides unique packages of insights and tools to complement what you have already wisely accumulated. For people who are just beginning this journey, this book introduces you to a whole new world of possibilities.

The vision for this book is the possibility of unleashing the power of shared thinking in the creative process. It is quite amazing to see ideas grow in the space best called the "shared mind" of two or twenty people collaboratively crafting, sketching, editing, and evolving fresh approaches to problems and opportunities in their work. It is this process that allows the impossible to become possible, the ordinary to become unparalleled.

Jack Ricchiuto
August 1996

Creative Opportunities

1 THE POWER OF AN IDEA

Nothing in nature is more fragile or more powerful than an idea.

Flying across the United States gives us a direct experience of the power of ideas. Every few minutes, our view of the landscape is punctuated by the sprawling web of a metropolitan area. Each city we see today began as an idea in the shared mind of a few people on an adventure. From that idea, families became communities and neighbors became markets. A tour of industrial parkways in any city is a tour of businesses that each started as an idea. Ideas have always had the power to transform resources and lives.

Ideas inspired democracy, the building of peace treaties, and the dismantling of nuclear warheads. Ideas brought us jazz, the music of the Beatles, Mozart, and the blues. Thanks to ideas, we can now revive people from cardiac arrest, cure once incurable diseases, and perform miracles in surgery suites. Ideas built the cathedrals of Europe, the gardens of Japan, and the pyramids of Egypt.

Everything in science, technology, and medicine today was once labeled "*impossible*." Connecting a computer in North Carolina to a textile machine in Thailand, congratulating a friend on a new project by phone at 30,000 feet, editing a document before it's printed, giving life to a child through the heart of another child. There was a time when experts considered each technically and financially impossible. Through ideas, they all became possible.

Ideas make things happen. They run the world; they run your life. If you want to understand anyone's life, look at her or his ideas. If your organization does anything faster, better, cheaper or easier this year, it will happen because of ideas. After all, an organization is only as good as it thinks.

Take every opportunity you have to be a part of inventing and reinventing whatever it takes to make your organization a better supplier, partner, and employer. Joining any creative effort connects you to one of the most powerful and unlimited resources in the world: *ideas.*

2 CREATIVITY: DEFINED & DEMYSTIFIED

An idea is creative to the degree that it is new and useful. In the creative process, we rearrange and redesign what already exists into something of value that has never existed before.

Take a brilliant 400 year old innovation that took the risk out of building 20 story commercial and residential structures: the flush toilet. The premier model rearranged available resources (pipes & fasteners) into an unprecedented and much appreciated innovation.

Xerography, the ancestor of the Xerox machine, combined inked glass, sulfur coated plates, paper, powder, and lamps into a solution that would transform the document copying process forever. The magic of creativity is the magic of reshaping the familiar into the unfamiliar.

Every piece of music is the new and useful combination of 12 tones. Without taking away from the sheer magic and pleasure of the variety, we can easily see that the only difference between a piece by Bach, Vivaldi, Gershwin, and Sting is the rearrangement of the same 12 notes. To creative people, the world is a palette of possibilities waiting to be reconfigured into something magically new and useful.

If you don't think you have what it takes to be creative, think again. Perhaps, without knowing it, you practice pure creativity every time you think how you would do something differently. You are being creative every time you alter a recipe, decide how a film or book could have ended better, or any time you second-guess the coaching decisions in this afternoon's game. The same creative process that produces great symphonies, inventions, and industry innovations is at work every time you take the "road not taken."

You will always have the ability to rearrange the world a little differently than anyone else. No one can process information and imagination in precisely the same way you do. Feed this potential until it becomes a passion and you will join the ranks of those you cherish as creative.

3 THE CREATIVITY EDGE

Creative organizations have the edge on every level of performance. They are more productive, efficient, profitable, and agile. Their capacity for thinking in new ways about old problems empowers them to outperform other suppliers to their markets. People in creative organizations tend to enjoy what they do because more of themselves are involved in the task. Teams that are creative move through projects and problems with greater speed and effectiveness than their less creative peers. As a result, creative organizations have an easier time becoming the supplier and employer of choice.

Organizations more obsessed with consistency than creativity are less adaptable to changes in their market and slower in responding to and creating opportunities internally and externally.

In the kind of dynamic markets we're seeing today, organizations are more at risk by staying the same than in doing things differently. This is a contrast to life as we knew it even a few years ago. In the "good old days", risk-taking and change were considered synonymous. These days, risk-taking and the status quo have the most in common. This is why everything is fair game for innovation and invention in creative organizations. Creative organizations have redefined what is "sacred" as that which is most new and useful—not that which is most traditional.

4 IDEAS IN THE INFORMATION AGE

Heidi and Alvin Toffler, futurists and authors of *Creating A New Civilization,* call this the Information Age. Information now has the kind of power that property had in the Agrarian Age and that money had in the Industrial Age. Creative organizations treat intellectual capital as more valuable than any other kind of resource. They know that if you have all the time and money in the world and not one idea on how to best invest it, all you are is a bank account with an open calendar.

In an Information economy, intellectual capital drives every other kind of basic requirement for success. This is true whether your organization is a publicly held company, a family business, school system or government office.

Creative organizations are always information-rich organizations. Information is important to the creative process in three ways:

1. *Information tells us where unmet needs and unexplored opportunities exist*

2. *Information tells us what's already failed and succeeded*

3. *Information tells us about the availability, capability, and limitations of resources.*

Information is an essential and ongoing resource in every creative process.

In the Information Age, we value information as the basis for the kind of intelligence and power we need for solving today's problems. From a creative perspective though, information has intelligence and power only when we treat it as a tool rather than as an objective. Information as an end in itself leads to the paralysis of analysis, input overload, and non-value-added reporting. As a tool, information leads to ideas.

Nobody knows this better than most innovative organizations around today. As the Tofflers put it, "The real value of companies like Compaq or Kodak, Hitachi or Seimens, depends more on the ideas, insights and information in the heads of their employees and in the data banks and patents these companies control than on the trucks, assembly lines and other physical assets they may have."

5 THE IMAGINATION EDGE

"Imagination is more important than knowledge."

Albert Einstein

Not too long ago, hospital staff simply provided comfort to infants with pneumonia until their inevitable relief through death. Research gave us an understanding of pneumonia. Imagination gave us treatments and cures.

Facts gave us an explanation for fatal heart attacks. In 1956, imagination gave inventor Wilson Greatbach the pacemaker that prevents the immeasurable losses of hundreds of thousands of people every year.

Imagination gives us the ability to rearrange and reinvent our world in new and potentially useful ways. Imagination involves seeing new versions of a service we provide or product we produce every day. It is seeing new ways to organize work and coordinate people. Imagination is the essential element of all vision statements that inspire organizational transformation and greatness. Imagination allows us to think in the brilliant _olors and dimensions of possibility that takes us well beyond the two dimensional world of data. Data allows us to see only within the scope of what has already occurred. Imagination allows us to see the world in ways it has never been seen before.

Don't forget to take your imagination to work, to your next conversation or meeting. More importantly, connect the limitless power of your imagination with people you live, work, and network with. Shared creativity has been the inspiring force behind more than a few outstanding innovations in just about any field you can name. Imagination is the most important tool to bring to any problem or project. It has the power to transform information into solutions and knowledge into wisdom.

6 IDEAS ARE LIVING THINGS

In biology class we learn the distinctions between "living" and "non-living." Where would you put ideas?

When you have an idea, you have something that is as alive as any seed, plant or rainforest. Ideas are breathing, pulsating potential in your mind or in conversation. When they sprout up in a fertile enough environment, even impractical and barely new ideas can evolve and grow into robust solutions to problems. Like infants of any species, ideas mature through continuous interdependency with other ideas, information, resources, and opportunities. Collaborative creativity outperforms individual creativity many times simply because the collaboration provides a richer context within which rich varieties of ideas can evolve and grow.

Most great innovations and artistic achievements evolved from fragile ideas. In many cases, mature ideas resemble their original inspirations about as much as people's retirement pictures resemble their baby pictures. At Inventure Place in Akron, Ohio, the home of the Inventor's Hall Of Fame, there is an early version of medical imaging equipment. Comparing that crude beginning to this year's model at Picker International, a leading innovator in medical imaging technology, provides a vivid and inspiring lesson in idea evolution.

In a study of the National Inventor's Hall Of Fame 1995 inductees, Harvard University researchers found that in some cases, it took 25 years of development to turn creative ideas into practical applications. As creativity researcher Weisberg puts it, "There is actually very little support for the notion that creative solutions to problems come about in flashes of insights." Great ideas evolve from good and mediocre ideas.

Kleenex is a good example of idea evolution. The idea of Kleenex evolved out of someone seeing the potential value of bandage supplies left over from World War I. Bandages were adapted and sold in retail markets as cold cream remover. Slow sales led to the idea of a market study, resulting in the discovery that Kleenex users had developed a new use for it—as a handkerchief substitute. This idea led to an ad campaign, "Don't put a cold in your pocket", that led to a dramatic increase in sales and the launching of brand innovation. Ideas are living things.

Glass artist, author and Kent State University art instructor, Henry Halem, tells stories of pieces that went through literally dozens of evolutions in the process of being designed and produced before the final form was successfully completed. The magic of the process is in how the ultimate artistic expressions that meet the requirements of the project only sometimes slightly resemble the original sparks of creativity.

The more you treat even your most fuzzy and fragile seed ideas as living things, the more creative ideas you will have. Don't expect every idea to come out of your head or out of any initial conversation fully formed. Expect to protect ideas from overexposure to toxic elements and to expose them to supportive and nurturing elements. Expect to shape and reshape, revise, and edit most ideas until they achieve the level of uniqueness and usefulness the situation requires. Working collaboratively almost guarantees idea evolution. Because they cannot bring your experience to the table, other people can only offer different versions and alternatives to what you originally cook up. For the same reasons, you can only do the same for them.

7 NEW IDEA CROSSING

New ideas can be born of data or imagination. Data-generated ideas tend to have the most initial support. Imagination-generated ideas can have at least as much if not more potential for new and unique solutions to problems. Give extra attention and support to the "madcap" ideas you encounter, discover or produce in your work. Do the same for ideas you are tempted to question or resist in a conversation or meeting. Because they are living things, ideas are not self-sustaining until they receive enough initial protection and nurturing.

If nothing else, write your idea down. People like Thomas Edison, with his hundreds of notebooks, give us lessons about the importance of keeping seed ideas around. You never know when you'll need them. Paper or discs can be more reliable storage and retrieval tools than any busy and overloaded memory.

The next time you see any new idea approaching the buzz of conversation traffic, slow down and protect these babies from being run over by everyone's big agendas and mature ideas. As living beings, new ideas cannot survive and develop on their own without your help in protecting and nurturing them along.

8 CREATIVITY OPPORTUNITIES

There are no limits to our opportunities for creativity. Creativity is important any time current resources or approaches are inadequate for getting the job done. Many problems today have no cookbook attached. Even many of the "proven" approaches from "best in class" organizations featured in cover stories defy simple duplication from one context to another. Successful applications require creative translations accommodating unique cultures, market differences, and organizational politics. If you're a leader in your market or industry, you may have no one to copy. Moving on means being creative and innovative.

With shrinking resources, spiraling customer expectations, and unprecedented problems and opportunities, creativity is the only viable bridge to achieving your strategic vision and goals.

Here are four common categories of opportunities for creativity in your work.

1. Improvements

Creativity is important any time we want to make something faster, better, cheaper or easier. Every improvement in performance begins with the creative process.

The idea of making things faster leads us to opportunities related to cycle time, set up time, turnaround time, lead time, and delays. Making things better is related to improved performance and results. Examples include improving sales per advertising dollar, miles per gallon, defects per batch, hospital days per case, graduates per program, and approvals per application. Making things cheaper reflect an emphasis on creative ways to decrease costs per product or service unit and decreases in the causes of costs including waste, scrap, returns, and rejects. Making things easier is a focus on userfriendliness.

Every opportunity for improvement is an opportunity for creativity. There are no new improvements without new ideas.

2. Innovations

Where improvement creates a value-added change in something that already exists, an innovation introduces something new that has never existed before. Velcro is a good example of innovation. It was not created as a better button, snap or string. It introduced a whole new approach to fasteners.

Other examples of innovations: dishwashers, the VCR, television, satellites, the fax, baseball, golf, baseball, penicillin, computers, and organ transplants. In health care, monitoring patient vital signs and symptoms has always been important to disease prevention and control. An interesting innovation involves technology that can transmit real-time health status information over the phone from the patient's home to their doctor's office. PVC was not developed as a better-cheaper version of metal-based pipe. It introduced a whole new set of pipe possibilities.

Improvements imply fixing what's broken. Innovations focus on inventing something that works in an entirely different way. In your next problem-solving meeting, be the voice of innovation. Get everyone outside the box of "logical" solutions. Be unapologetically bold in suggesting a whole new approach to the problem that's guaranteed to raise the eyebrows of at least the traditionalists in the group. Be unapologetically brave in asking questions that challenge the very assumptions on which "logical" solutions seem to be based. Be the one who asks questions that tempts the group into thinking of an approach to the situation that would make the traditionalists' heads spin. Why not? Who knows where it may lead? Remember: most great ideas end up looking only vaguely similar to their original version.

3. Conflict Resolution

Solutions to conflicts always require new ideas. Conflicts persist to the degree that we fail to cook up ideas that can win consensus. Conflicts are the convergence of ideas that are unable to win consensus. They persist to the degree that we become divided by option restrictive either-or thinking. It is a myth that conflicts are inevitable when the resources "pie only has so many pieces." The root cause of many conflicts is not a difference but a lack of new and useful ideas. Differences in creative teams spark and stimulate richer options and alternatives.

Differences become conflicts when we have not been creative enough to invent new and useful ways to meet or exceed our different needs.

Groups always have differences. In creative groups, differences take the group beyond individual capabilities to new levels of possibility. In uncreative groups, differences polarize and paralyze the group from completing even the most simple task.

Many conflicts represent contradictory requirements—trying to come up with a solution that is at the same time:

- New *and* nonthreatening
- High tech *and* high touch
- Unprecedented *and* noncontroversial
- Inexpensive *and* high quality
- Expensive *and* competitive
- Flexible *and* consistent
- Proven *and* innovative

Meeting contradictory criteria in the same product or service requires creative solutions. Unless a group is creative, it will suffer from chronic conflicts that prevent progress, sap energies and waste valuable resources. Creativity allows any group to turn differences into strengths.

4. Marketing Solutions

We even need to be creative about how we package, sell, support, and deal with resistance to our ideas. When you present a radically different idea, you're likely to get a lesson in how few ideas sell themselves. The successful selling of ideas requires the invention of attractive packaging, positioning, and advertising.

It takes creativity to describe complex solutions simply and convey the benefits of ideas that go against the grain of convention. It takes innovation to capture interest, support and approval of ideas. This is no small task when your market or audience is ambivalent, resistant, politically influenced, misinformed, unimaginative or closed-minded.

The only times we don't need to be creative are those that require formula responses to situations. In these situations, we don't need ideas, just recipes. The moment we need an improvement, innovation, resolution or marketing solution, we need to be creative.

9 CREATIVITY CHALLENGED SOLUTIONS

Because a solution is trendy or traditional, it may not necessarily be creative. By definition, ideas must be both new and useful to qualify as creative and innovative.

Take benchmarking—the practice of comparing your practices against best practices in other organizations and industries. Benchmarking can be a brilliant tool for stimulating fresh thinking in your team. It can also be a barrier to creativity if it means directly importing tools that work in other organizations without creative adjustments to your unique purposes and context.

"Proven" (Me-too)" solutions and "That's the way our ancestors did it" paradigms can be major barriers to innovation in organizations. They can also be great opportunities for creativity. You are creative when you adapt and reinvent any tool to achieve your team's goals.

Here is a short list of creatively challenged trends and traditions.

- Layoffs
- Suggestion boxes
- Restructuring
- Competing on price
- Management training
- Idea contests
- Top-down goal setting
- Quality slogans
- Reengineering

If you've experimented with any of these and found the results not meeting expectations, it may be an indicator that you need something a lot more creative, or at least a more creative application of the original "model." The next chance you have, get some people together to reinvent anything that your organization has embraced as "the" answer to (this month's) crisis.

10 BREAKTHROUGHS

In the past 15 years, the natural sciences have produced paradigm-busting research challenging commonly accepted assumptions about competition in nature. Biologist and author Robert Augros summarizes the current understanding. He says that "Because each species has its own niche and its own task, fights between animals of different species are exceedingly rare, if they occur at all."

Animals use niches as an efficient alternative to costly competition. They create feeding niches by choosing times, methods, and locations different from others sharing the same geography and resources.

The applications to innovation in any business are unlimited. It is far more innovative to create a market (niche) for a new kind of product or service than it is to compete against other suppliers for the same market. Compared to trying to beat others at the same game, niching is a superior strategy because we are creating the games others must play.

A breakthrough is a deliverable that creates its own market. 3M's Post It Notes was a breakthrough. Before Post It Notes, there was no Post It Note market for 3M to compete within. 3M created this market with this innovative breakthrough. Other breakthroughs include Sony's Walkman, the CAT Scan, the microwave oven, Federal Express and the compact disk.

Howard Johnson's is a good example of a breakthrough. It became the first restaurant franchise, the first turnpike restaurant and the first chain of look-and-taste-alikes. As a break-through business, it enjoyed the role of this distinction by being able to set the rules and standards by which all followers must follow just to play in the game.

Breakthroughs are prototypical examples of innovation at work. In most cases, the innovators weren't interested in competing with existing solutions to problems. They focused their creative imaginations on whole new solutions that in many cases replaced existing approaches.

A breakthrough is an important kind of creative opportunity in markets that have become outgrown, narrow or competitive beyond your resources. Keep your eye on breakthrough opportunities in your business.

11 TOOLS FOR IDENTIFYING OPPORTUNITIES

Here are three powerful tools organizations are using today to identify opportunities for innovation.

1. Customer Surveys

When they are well-designed, customer surveys can tell us what problems can be best leveraged into new levels of customer satisfaction, sales or profitability. When surveys are live, the dialogue can even get customers' suggestion ideas that we, from our non-customer perspective, could never have.

Here are two questions that can evoke creative opportunities:

■ *What, if fixed, could lead to increased returns and referrals?*

■ *What needs are not being met by anyone in our industry or field?*

Changes in perspectives mean changes in ideas. If you want new ideas, ask people who have different perspectives—

especially your own customers. How many times have you (as someone's customer) thought how a better to end a film, prepare a restaurant dish, design a car or word the directions to an "easy-to-assemble" contraption? Chances are that those on the supplier end of those products and services may have never had the ideas you had.

2. Process Mapping

In process mapping, we visually display all of the steps and their relationships in a work process. A process map shows exactly what tends to happen from the beginning to the end of some process in our work. With enough attention to detail, we can discover dozens of opportunities to make things go faster, better, cheaper or easier.

- Bottlenecks
- Disconnects in the flow of information
- Delays & glitches in handoffs
- Redundancies
- Functions begging for automation
- Automation begging for updates & simplification
- Non-value-added steps, waste & scrap

3. Benchmarking

In benchmarking, we're comparing ourselves to the best in class. Every organization has functions that can be done better, faster, better, and cheaper.

Many of these functions occur in fields other than your own. Inventory control is a function that occurs in manufacturing, health care and education. Sales and marketing functions also cut across industries, as does customer complaint handling. Chances are, the "best in class" and best-in-other-class organizations have achieved levels of performance beyond your own. Their lessons learned can motivate your organization's perspective on creative opportunities.

Benchmarking not only tells us where opportunities exist, it can give us fresh and innovative approaches. Since ideas can come from anywhere, benchmarking puts us closer to innovations waiting to work in our own backyard.

12 LOOK AGAIN

If you think you've located the opportunities for creativity in your work, look again. They are not always obvious. For three people, the same problem can be an opportunity for excuses, overtime or creativity. Creative opportunities do not come in specially marked packages.

It is possible to miss a creative opportunity looking you right in the eye. It is with great frustration that people read about a fortune made on something they "could have come up with." Here are two mindsets that can blind anyone to creative opportunities.

1. Management By Hope

This is hoping things get better on their own. From this perspective, we live by slogans like, "Time heals" and "We'll cross that bridge when we get there." Management by hope is a missed opportunity to do some creative thinking right now.

2. Commitment To Cynicism

This is believing things won't get better no matter what we do. This mindset is full of itself. Nothing knows more than cynicism. Unfortunately, it becomes a self-fulfilling prophecy. Cynicism never sees creative opportunities, and as a result always gets to be right about their never happening.

Although moments of hope and cynicism can be handy pain-management tools in a dilemma, never use them as excuses for missing opportunities to be inventive.

13 The Benefits Of Innovation

International creativity expert Edward de Bono says that "There can be no doubt that creativity is the most important human resource of all. Without creativity, there would be no progress at all."

Over the past few decades, Japan's technology-producing companies have not been slouches in the business of product innovation. They dug around in American and European techno-garbage cans and have come up with things like tape recorders, TV's, VCR's and quartz watches. In each case, Japanese product developers applied their collective imaginations to products deemed unsuccessful by their originators, ultimately transforming them into market dominating innovations.

As *Innovate Or Evaporate* author James Higgins points out, "Most of Japan's firms have already begun replacing a product the moment it enters the marketplace." Those of us hoping to get the latest technology know this. As soon as we get our prized model out of the box, we're reading about the next generation promising more, better, cheaper, and faster.

Toyota is obsessed with innovation and its rewards. In a section of its 1994 annual report, entitled "How We Saved $1.5 Billion," Toyota lists some of the creative ideas from employees that added up to this impressive ledger achievement.

- Smoothing out jagged holes for wiring in body panels
- Reducing the parts used in turn signals from 20 to 7
- Designing new vehicles compatible with existing parts
- Reducing administrative paperwork
- Reducing automation

As it became the #1 computer supplier in 1995, Compaq decided to radically reinvent its already successful assembly process. Why break and redesign what's already working? Because the people at Compaq developed the ideas on how to, and the rewards for innovation seemed too good to pass by.

14 WINDOWS OF OPPORTUNITIES

The next meeting you attend where the group is struggling is an opportunity for you and them to be creative together. The next problem a customer hands you may be begging for fresh alternatives and solutions. The next time you get a "no" to a request or proposal, you will have a prime opportunity to be creative.

Don't be surprised if your work (and life) begins to look like one series of opportunities to be creative after another. The window of creativity is always open.

Being Creative

15 WHAT MAKES CREATIVE PEOPLE CREATIVE?

Creativity expert Robert Weisberg has come to the conclusion that "Creative individuals possess no extraordinary characteristics—basically, they do what we are all capable of doing."

In a creativity seminar a few years ago, a group of people self-described as noncreative were asked to think of interesting ways to redesign common products like umbrellas. New possibilities emerged. Maybe handles can be temperature-sensitive—getting warm for cold hands or cool for warm hands. Maybe small lights or sound systems can be built into the top underside. Or maybe James Bond-inspired personal safety features can be installed into the tip.

This is the inventive mind at work—putting together the familiar in unfamiliar ways. According to engineer/science writer Tom Logsdon, "Creativity is the ability to perceive connections between things that are not obviously connected." Whether we practice or avoid creativity in our work, we all have this basic ability. Those who take a more creative approach to their work tend to be those who have spent the most time practicing it.

Art teachers tell us that the people who produce the best art, films, and writing today had to learn to become inventive and innovative. Learning the technical aspects of a craft does not automatically lead to creativity. Creativity is something you cultivate.

Internationally known German born artist Claus Moje loves the challenge of teaching art students in Sydney, Australia. According to Claus, art students do not come in the door fully equipped with the basic competencies required to do the kind of creative work they produce for their senior show. These kinds of competencies evolve out of persistent instruction, coaching and practice.

As creativity consultant, Charles Thompson, says, "Creativity is not so much a personality trait or talent as it is a process." Artists, inventors, designers, and writers spend more time in the creative process than people who might complain that they aren't "creative enough." Creativity is not an internal organ you're either born with or not.

For award winning artist, Charlotte Lees, "Creativity is something you have to constantly exercise." She says that "What separates us [creative people] from noncreative people is that we constantly exercise that part of our brain that forces us to use our imagination." This exercise of imagination is obvious in the amazing sculpted and painted structures she designs for residential and commercial installations.

Creative people simply *do* more creativity. That's what makes them more creative. Forget about being creative only when your resource back is against the wall. Creative practice reflects a creative lifestyle. Practice creative thinking especially when there is no immediate pressure or payoff. When you and a few people are exploring approaches to a problem or opportunity, make a habit of offering different alternatives to the ones already on the table. Start treating creativity as a developable skill.

16 CREATIVITY MYTHS

As a word in the English language, "creativity" didn't even exist until the 1870's. For a long time, creativity was wrapped in mystery as a divinely inspired or genetically determined gift that one was either graced with or not.

Even today, creativity is still subject to much mythology. This is due in part to our lack of education about the creative process, and in part to our lack of interaction with people who make a living as artists, designers, and inventors.

Here are just a few of the misperceptions we have about creative people:

Myth 1: They are experts in their field—brighter than us

According to Edward De Bono, "Lack of education is possibly the most potent mechanism for the production of breakaway ideas." Paradigm shift master of ceremonies, Joel Barker, suggests that when we have a really impossible problem to solve, we show them to customers and new hires...the ones "who don't know what can't be done."

Myth 2: They have the money to be creative

Two of the greatest innovators in any business, much less the ice cream business, started Ben and Jerry's during the peak of the get-trim frenzy. Their idea was to offer people ice cream they couldn't resist. Their hugely innovative, successful, and socially responsible business started with $8,000 and an ice cream correspondence course from Penn State. How's that for the power of ideas in the information age?

Myth 3: They have a lot of freedom within which to work

Charlotte Lees, talking about her innovative life figures sculpted in ways that defy simple description, says, "The more restrictions I have, the more creative I am." It is unlikely that

Mozart sat around whining that he only had the same 12 notes as he did for his last concerto.

Myth 4: Their ideas just come to them out of nowhere

Go to gallery talks by successful artists. Ask where they got their ideas for a piece and check your watch. It will likely be more than a few minutes of their talking about this trip and that conversation and some research they once did, and, and, and ...

As living things, ideas grow, evolve and give birth to new generations of ideas. They grow out of experiences and information, successes, and failures. Choreographer Martha Graham: "I am a thief...I steal from the best where it happens to be—Plato, Picasso." Many great innovations grew out of previous generations of innovations. The "new sound" of the Beatles in the 1960's clearly reflected their roots in earlier music forms. Nothing comes from nothing. For many designers, inspiration and imagination is not the product of a blank page or work table, but an active dialogue between the designer and interesting examples of design in a variety of artistic and natural contexts.

Today's top innovators are collaborators. Award winning ideas come out of the collaborative evolution from one idea, one piece of information, one insight to the next. More and better ideas have the chance of coming out of three or thirty shared minds than out of any one.

Myth 5: They are spontaneous—No Franklin Planners

Brent Young, one of the 1994 winners of the Cleveland Museum Of Art's invitational May Show and founder of the Cleveland Art Institute's Glass program says that over 90% of his process in working with the very challenging, dynamic process of hot glass is planned.

Behavioral researchers Jacob Getzels & Mihalyi Csikszentmihalyi did a study of 31 art students in the mid-

1970's. They found more originality in drawings from students who do more planning and changing than from students who try to be more spontaneous and committed to their initial spontaneous productions. The most creative art students considered a large number of possibilities before deciding on their final selection for drawings. They tend to do more planning before drawing and do more editing than their less creative peers as they go. So much for creative people being wild and spontaneous.

17 BEGINNER'S MIND

"If your mind is empty, it is always ready for anything; it is open to everything. In the beginner's mind there are many possibilities; in the expert's mind there are few."

Zen Teacher, Shunryu Suzuki

18 "AND WHAT COLOR ARE YOUR CLOUDS, JACK?"

Though we all have the ability to be creative, some people have developed their ability more than others.

We can trace our lack of creativity to lessons we learned early in our development. In many ways, we were trained to be uncreative. This is not a criticism; our parents and teachers worked hard to give us what they were taught to believe and think.

"The directions say to select only the one right answer"
"Now, make sure you stay in the lines"
"I'll ask the questions here"
"No, I'm sorry but that is not a word"
"Class, what color is the sky? And what color are your clouds, Jack?"

Maybe the "official sky" is due north at a bright blue mid-day. Maybe your sky was west at a brilliant yellow-orange sunset or east at a delicate pink rose dawn.

Many creative people did well in school. They picked the right answer and colored the right sky within the lines. There is much evidence that creative people respect facts and rules. After all, everything creative is as practical as it is novel.

There is however always another side to creative people in school. They suspect something peculiarly interesting in the "wrong" answers, the "wrong" solutions, and the "wrong" colors. They have somehow developed an intuitive sense that there may be something of immeasurable value in the road not taken.

So if you don't think you're as creative as you'd like to be or need to be, stop beating yourself up about it. Your creative potentials have been limited by the dualistic true-false, either-or, right-wrong world you were trained to see. While you're at it, stop beating up other people for being uncreative. They didn't invent the unimaginative life either. Instead, spend more time practicing and encouraging creativity. The possibilities are endless.

19 THE 4 CORE CREATIVITY COMPETENCIES

Brainstorming is, for most of us, the only exposure we get to anything "creative." Compared to how many successful artists and inventors *actually* work, brainstorming is an over-simplified caricature of their creative process. As it is usually taught and practiced, brainstorming typically requires only that we download onto paper or screens ideas that may or may not have regard for implementation requirements. The process rarely encourages more subtle and powerful practices like challenging commonly-held assumptions, defying logic and integrating critical thinking throughout the inventive process.

The actual creative process of artists and inventors typically involves four core competencies—being innovative, open-minded, provocative and practical.

The more you practice and integrate these four skills into your creative process, the more potential you will have in being creative and innovative. If your preference (or requirement) is to work creatively with other people, you will find that each of us is stronger in one area than another. Few of us are equally strong in all four competencies. For this reason, we are always more creative together than we could ever be apart. Creativity in isolation is possible. Collaborative creativity takes us to new levels of possibility we can never quite fully anticipate, imagine or measure.

1. Being Open-minded

Quantum physics has given us two profoundly interesting and important insights into the nature of reality.

1. Actuality and potentiality are equally real.
2. The essential difference between actuality and potentiality is a matter of perspective.

For someone preparing a report, a piece of paper fresh out of the printer is actually a document. To someone else, the same piece of paper is potentially a coffee cup coaster or funnel. At the same time, paper has these two equally real qualities of actuality and potentiality. The difference between the two? One can be seen by the senses, the other only by the imagination.

When we look at things with the eyes of our imagination, failed products inspire market breakthroughs and abandoned buildings inspire award-winning renovations. Open-mindedness is the ability to see the potential side of actual. It is the ability to see how one group's garbage can become another group's garden.

The opposite of open-mindedness is attachment to our senses. It is what *Quantum Healing* author Deepak Chopra refers to as the "materialism of the senses." Our culture uses the senses as the ultimate measure of reality. If you can count it, smell it, weigh it, observe it, we say it is "real." We even say that if you can only imagine it, it is not real.

The senses however do not always provide us with a reliable test for reality. Our senses tell us that the cursor blinking in the same spot on a screen is not moving, when in fact, as an object on this planet, it is moving at dizzying speeds. Our senses tell us that the earth is flat, when it is so curved, you can only see a fraction of it from any one place on it. Our senses tell us that there is only one galaxy, when we now know that there are at least 40 billion galaxies.

We have to remember that our senses by design filter out information. Our senses create one version of the world by excluding all others. In the world of the senses, reality is always a matter of perspective. This explains why ten people in a meeting can describe the same problem in at least ten different ways. Organizational development consultant and innovator Margaret Wheatley says she has developed a practice of no longer arguing with people about what is real.

Open-mindedness takes us beyond the world created by our senses. We practice open-mindedness when we are curious. The core of open-mindedness is curiosity: curiosity about the causes of a problem beyond the obvious ones first presented to us, curiosity about both sides of a decision, dilemma or conflict.

Open-mindedness expects that there are up sides to "bad" ideas and down sides to "good" ideas. Open-mindedness is curiosity about how to use scrap, waste, and outdated equipment in ways we've never imagined. Open-mindedness is curiosity about how to take a half-baked, unpopular or unfeasible idea and craft it into something fairly workable.

Creative people approach life with an open, inclusive mind. Even after they make snap decisions, they still keep their minds totally open to the possibility of other options to consider for future opportunities and enhancements. Open-mindedness is an essential ingredient in the ability to see new ways of solving problems.

2. Being Inventive

Invention is play with possibilities, alternatives and variations. Inventive people are delighted to go beyond the tried, true, and proven. They don't believe that the usual approach to a problem is the only approach—that we're limited to or by the norm. They're always asking or thinking, *"What else....?"*

In open-mindedness, we practice detachment from our senses—detachment from our first impressions. In inventiveness, we practice detachment from our first ideas.

First ideas are usually logical ideas. Watch a not particularly inventive group of people approach any problem or new opportunity. Most of their initial ideas are in the realm of acceptable because most fall within the range of not-too-different from the norm.

Inventive people on the other hand, are intrigued with the world of the different, unfamiliar, and uncommon. They have no commitment to traditional, trendy or well-tested approaches to problems. Their commitment is to invent something that has never been thought, much less tried, before. Inventive people are always more interested in their fifth or tenth idea than they are their first or second. The more ideas a group has, the further the group gets from the familiar, and the closer it gets to new, unique, and different.

Invention is the question, "What else?" *What else* could bring about better communication? *What else* could make working here more satisfying, interesting, fun or rewarding? *What else* can reduce wait times? *What else* can decrease unnecessary costs? Creative groups are always interested in reinventing things—even if for no other reason than for the sheer challenge, joy or pleasure intrinsic to the process of inventing.

Inventive people use their first ideas as springboards to more possibilities—as paths not destinations. As Albert Einstein put it, creativity "comes to you when you get out of your own way." This translates into getting out of the way of the old and useful to the new, interesting, and even more useful.

When we're being inventive, we are by definition, developing ideas that may have little initial support. Inventing always pushes our imagination's envelope far past our familiarity zones. It is at the same time, nervy, and exciting.

3. Being Provocative

Edward de Bono was once asked to facilitate an idea session with engineers at a large aircraft company. The group needed fresh ideas for airplane safety.

Realizing that this group had a difficult time being creative together, de Bono decided to use provocation to get them to be open-minded and inventive. He suggested the following provocation:

PLANES SHOULD FLY UPSIDE DOWN

In most groups, this would spark criticism, ridicule, and questions. How would you work the drinks? How would passengers like it? De Bono patiently facilitated them into a more open-minded and inventive approach. He got them talking about the potential advantages of the idea.

This lead to the possibility that the flight crew might be able to see the underside of the plane during flights—a strategic advantage related to wheels, birds, ice, and wing conditions. De Bono then asked, "How else could you create this kind of advantage?"

The group's thinking evolved into the idea of placing small cameras at specific positions under the plane, feeding information to cockpit screens. This became a breakthrough idea in the group's approach to improving the safety of commercial airplanes.

Sometimes we can only get to fresh ideas through provocative ones. The psychology behind provocation is simple. When we approach a problem, our mind is designed to serve up pictures of how similar problems were solved in the past. Sometimes, the only way to break out of these patterns is by introducing a provocation that forces us into thinking in new ways, creating altogether new patterns.

The ability to jump tracks in our thinking is called lateral thinking, a term Edward de Bono coined. It has become the basis for solutions to all kinds of business, educational, and international problems in the past several years. The success of Ed Deming in Japan, the US and around the world is based in large part to the provocation he used to spark a revolution in thinking and management practices.

Provocative questions invite us to explore the land of the impossible, where all great discoveries ultimately occur. How do we change tooling set-ups without tools? How do we process orders in a completely paperless system? How do we build roads that fix their own cracks?

If you were in a group charged with the task of coming up with the concept and design for air bags, you could start off with the provocative question: "How could we make cars more safe by making sure people get hit in the face every time a head-on collision occurs?" This one question could very likely lead you to the breakthrough idea of airbags.

4. Being Practical

By definition, if an idea isn't practical, it isn't creative. Different isn't creative unless it serves some purpose. Successful artists, inventors, designers, and writers always work with purpose—whether our purposes sustain or evolve through the creative process. They tend to do a lot of research to clarify the requirements and constraints of opportunities and resources. They use these factors to spark and refine new options in the creative process.

The final phase of their creative process is seeing an idea "work." Not just on paper, in theory, or with the model—but in the field, in real time, where it counts.

Being practical translates into looking for interesting ways to work within the constraints of the situation. In every creative endeavor, the materials and resources of our process always have both capabilities and constraints. When we're creative, we are constantly researching and experimenting. We know from experience that in the end, everything must work. Practical is not an option for the artist or inventor—it is an obligation and opportunity.

When architects design a wonderfully fresh look and feel to a space, they are keenly interested in the compatibility, durability and flexibility of materials used to sculpt that space into angles, curves and lines. When TV advertising writers want to inform and entertain a market with a specific idea, they are always researching and testing the elements that must be used to achieve the specific impact required.

To be practical is to be continuously interested in and dedicated to user requirements, implementation constraints, and the conditions for success.

Creativity also means paying attention to details, planning, research, and testing. Creative people know from experience that original ideas often require some change, adaptation, and adjustments based on the conditions of implementation and installation.

Just ask any assembly line person struggling with a new piece of equipment or tooling developed by engineers without the end-user's voice in mind. It often takes their practical insights to get the thing working right. New ideas become useful ideas when we spend enough time and energy solving the (secondary) implementational problems that invariably emerge in any creative process.

In any creative process, being practical is at least as important as being provocative, inventive and open-minded. It is having a bias for details and action.

20 CREATIVITY INDICATORS

Here are 7 indicators that you are being creative in your team and organization:

1. You question assumptions others simply treat as fact

2. You spend more time thinking up alternatives to ideas that don't fly, than you do trying to coerce and convert others to your initial ideas

3. You suggest win-win ideas that have the most likelihood to serve divergent opinions, needs, and agendas

4. You suggest "wild and crazy" ideas just to get other people out of a rut

5. You raise practical, political or end-user concerns that no one else seems to be voicing

6. You suggest benefits to ideas you may not automatically like and disadvantages to ideas you may like

7. You maintain a durable expectation that every problem is solvable.

21 PREMATURE COGNITIVE COMMITMENTS

Creative people are first and last, paragons of paradox. They are as curious as they are evaluative and as practical as they are imaginative. Because the creative process demands it, creative people strive to be serious and playful, imaginative and practical, evaluative and intensely curious. The same can be said for creative groups, whether they are informally gathered over coffee or formally assembled for multiphase projects, whether they involve two, twenty or two hundred people.

One thing they are not? Limited. Creative people and groups limit their thinking to the size of the universe. Nothing is outside the bounds of potentially inspiring, stimulating or informing the ideas we need to meet the creative opportunities greeting us daily.

Deepak Chopra, talking about effective living, suggests that to live up to our fullest creative potentials, we avoid what are perhaps the most insidious limits on our thinking—"premature cognitive commitments."

These are the mindsets that occur in all insect, animal, and mammal species. If you separate a fish tank into two sections with a glass divider for a few weeks, the fish will develop a rule that says, "Don't cross this line." A few weeks after removing the divider, you will notice the fish still swimming to but not beyond the space where the divider was.

Put fleas in a jar and a lid on the jar. Let the fleas develop a mental rule about not going beyond the lid, then remove the lid and watch the fleas stay inside the lidless jar.

Tie a young elephant to a twig with a light string until it learns to stay in place. When it gets to be an adult, tie it to a large tree with a strong chain and watch it pull the tree loose. Then tie it to a small tree with a light string and watch it go nowhere.

Tell people what "*can*" and "*can't*" be done and watch how many new ideas they have. These are premature cognitive commitments. If you want to be creative, avoid them. Treat all perceived barriers as porous and permeable, and you will find yourself being more creative than you ever imagined possible.

Physicist David Bohm puts it this way. "Genius in fact involves sufficient energy and passion to question assumptions that have been taken for granted over long periods."

What are your assumptions about your creative potentials or the potentials of a group you're in? Do you assume that your potentials are inadequate given the scope and size of problems you're trying to solve? Are you assuming that creativity requires having "enough" time, resources or support?

Be careful about taking your assumptions too seriously—especially if they are supported by "data" from your senses. Remember the intrinsic limitations of the senses and the power of premature cognitive commitments. Approach every conversation, every brainstorming session, and problem-solving meeting with a beginner's mind. Practice open-mindedness, be inventive and play with provocative possibilities. Nothing could be more practical. In the land of unlimited possibility, genius is born.

22 CREATIVE OVERFLOW

When you practice the four core creativity competencies in any area of your work or life, there is often overflow into other areas. Open-mindedness and inventiveness, practiced in the kitchen over time flows into our approach to problems and opportunities at work.

Becoming more creative in any area of your life will therefore revitalize your capacity for creativity in all other areas. The same is true for organizations. Creative sparks from one team, one project or one problem can fly and ignite creative thinking in other areas. Remember your spark-like, fractal potentials the next time you venture into new territory in a project or problem-solving conversation in the hallway, in the field with customers or on the shop floor.

Creating Together

23 THE PHYSICS OF COLLABORATION

Quantum physics today gives us a much different picture of ourselves and our world than Newtonian physics did a century ago. The Newtonian world was a world of separate things. Oxford science lecturer and writer, Diane Zohar, sums up the quantum perspective by saying that, "The whole notion of 'separate' has no basis in reality."

This has no small implication for those of us who are obsessed with being creative and innovative in our work. If nothing in the universe is separate, the only way to create in harmony with the nature of things is to create together.

Physicist David Bohm puts his spin on life in a quantum world: "When you see the world and yourself through the eyes of a quantum perspective, you begin to see that "everything is interconnected." Organizational consultant Margaret Wheatley captures the essence of this perspective by saying that "Every living organism exists...by embracing the environment and understanding that there is no boundary between itself and the environment." This helps explain why creative ideas thrive in boundaryless organizations—organizations dedicated to removing boundaries between people, functions, and resources.

Organizations designed from an understanding of this dramatic breakthrough in physics tend to focus on things like functional integration, seamlessness, teamwork, and collaboration. It is a world where we practice a clear bias for shared ideas and opportunities. It is a world where we work hard to keep people connected—especially when they are trying to be open-minded, inventive, provocative, and practical. If the universe works as wonderfully as it does because everything works together, what other possible way should we approach the creative process?

If your thinking has kept up with physics from the last century to this, you are most likely working hard to build partnerships with your internal and external suppliers and customers. You're attending more meetings and sharing more projects with people previously referred to as "them." You're doing more networking and creating political alliances in a month than your grandparents perhaps did in an entire career.

Why is it important that we collaborate? Because we're indivisibly connected. Whether we act like it or not, being and acting connected is our nature. Connecting our minds in the process of inventing and reinventing our business leverages this potential.

24 COLLABORATION IN NATURE

It is always awesome to see birds flying in formation across the morning sky. Nature is very efficient in its designs; there is zero waste in nature. Flying together, 25 birds can have 70% more range than a lone bird.

In the Bahamas, 300 small fish work together as a well orchestrated cleaning crew inside the mouths of larger fish, helping the client fish live longer due to fewer bacterial infections. The large client fish never eat their cleaning crew for lunch. This interdependency is a partnership of shared responsibility and rewards.

Psuedomyrnex ants of Central America keep harmful insects away, prune vines and shrubbery to keep them from crowding the growth of the Acacia plant that provides nutrients for ant larvae. Each optimizes the other's job security, quality of life, and development.

African birds called Honeyguides and badgerlike Ratels team up to eat bee products. Honeyguides scout out the best hives and tell the Ratel about locations and other operational details. The Ratel opens the hive for the honey it needs, allowing the Honeyguide to get the wax from the comb it needs.

These are just a few of endless examples of collaboration in nature. In each case, more problems are solved together than they could be solved apart.

In *The New Biology*, researcher Robert Augros tells us that "competition in natural conditions is rare." Collaboration is our quantum nature; to act otherwise requires special training and a particularly unevolved political environment.

25 WHAT ABOUT COMPETITION?

With an unquestioned respect for competition in business, we assume that competition is responsible for the continuous variety of quality products and services that consumers take for granted. We assume that competition "brings out the best" in all of us.

This thinking has traditionally influenced the design of organizations. We promote and reward internal competition for projects, work, and resources. We give prizes for the ideas documenting the biggest cost savings. We give perks and raises to those who meet their individual goals, whether or not they prevented other functions from reaching theirs.

But is the value of competition myth or reality?

Researcher Perry Buffington summarizes a ton of research on competition that most of us have never been exposed to. He says that "Scientists who consider themselves cooperative tend to have more published articles than their competitive colleagues. Cooperative business people have higher salaries. From elementary grades to college, cooperative students have higher grade point averages. Personnel directors who work together have fewer job vacancies to fill."

If this isn't enough, he goes on to say that "Not surprisingly, cooperation increases creativity."

Why is that?

- Cooperation between diverse perspectives gives us more different idea possibilities
- All of us bring more information and resources to the table than any one of us
- Because ideas require implementation, cooperation in idea-building means cooperation downstream.

Competition has downsides. According to *No Contest* author Alfie Kohn:

1. Competition promotes conformity

In competition, we try to beat apples with better apples rather than with oranges, a fruit, fruit drink or innovative fruit product no one has ever tasted before. Being "better than" can distract us from being different and unique.

2. Competition promotes risk aversion

Competition guarantees that there will be winners and losers. The fewer guarantees we have for winning in a competition, the more we risk in losing. When we compete, we stay away from the different and imaginative because it presents more risks. We stay less creative. When we're not competing, we have nothing to lose to competitors. With less to lose, we automatically feel more freedom to try new things, take smart risks and experiment with new approaches.

3. Competition distracts from creativity

The more time we spend trying to stay one better than the competition, the more we are tempted to take the low road of quickly copying whatever trend is hot this month. The more time we spend trying to copy, the less time we spend trying to create.

Add to this list, more costs of competition described by *TechnoTrends* author and futurist, Daniel Burrus.

- Losing sight of customers
- Focusing on the short-term
- Creating a reactive culture

In a creativity seminar recently, an automobile assembly line worker described how competition impacts her ability to be collaborative in her creative process. In her plant, creativity suffers from management by contest. Those with the "best" ideas win the "best" cash prizes.

The culture of competition presents a clear picture of what happens when collaboration goes unrewarded. When her peer employees have good ideas and give them to their foremen or engineers, rarely are employees credited for ideas they suggested or inspired. If you talk to fellow employees about your ideas, you run the same risk of someone "stealing" your idea and the potential bonus for cost savings.

She's describing a competitive culture where few ideas are expressed, creating little opportunity for the kinds of collaborations that are imperative for idea evolution. As she puts it, "You never tell anyone if you have an idea, because you don't know what they'll do with it."

Contrast this with what happens at the successful children's clothing catalogue, Biobottoms, Inc. Cofounder Joan Cooper credits some of the secret to their success to networking with competitor companies sharing her niche. She hosts cocktail parties in order to trade mailing lists, customer-vendor strategies and other innovations. It is the story of cooperation. Everyone shares—everyone wins. Look at what happens at Ohio's Honda plant where intrinsic rewards for innovation propel a truly best in class record for employee ideas submitted and used.

We are just beginning to discover what the world of business, creativity, and profits through innovations could be like when the quantum-oriented abundance-philosophy of cooperation replaces the Newtonian-based scarcity philosophy of competition.

Ironically, the most creative and innovative ideas in many organizations cannot be traced back to any single individuals. True collaboration makes individual recognition less and less possible.

26 MORE LESSONS FROM SCHOOL: WHY WE DON'T COLLABORATE

Collaboration requires that we share opportunities, responsibilities, resources, and ideas. For most of us, school was one injunction against collaboration after another.

"Do your own work"
"Get back to your desk and stay there"
"Do not copy"
"You must do your own homework/exam"
"No, I don't want anyone helping you with that"
"Everyone will get their own grade"
"If I find you sharing answers, your parents will be called"

When you read this list and remember the stern, dramatic tones that accompanied them, keep in mind that there were a lot of kids sitting around you who took it all in as religion. In time, they came to believe that problem-solving is best done when you've separated yourself from the rest of your world.

Of course we were all lectured in the virtues of getting along and helping our neighbor, but when it counted (on exams and assignments) we were not rewarded in action for collaborating.

If people are reluctant to work collaboratively in problem-solving, remember that this goes back a long way. It is not about you; it's not even about them. It is about what they got from people who passed along precisely what they got. If you want to help people be more collaborative—especially in problem-solving—start out with a clear understanding of how the world looks to them.

The next time you invite (or challenge) people to work together on a problem or opportunity, keep in mind that you may be asking them to go well beyond the limits of their learned comfort zone. If you see that of look of panic in their eyes, be kind. But be persistent. Without your encouragement and enthusiasm, it may be unlikely for them to discover the boundless world of collaboration awaiting them.

27 THE MEDIOCRITY MYTH

There is a misunderstanding that being creative together breeds mediocrity. The logic: If we only create and ultimately accept ideas that win consensus, we'll only create and accept mediocre ideas.

Because being creative means coming up with different ideas, we are less likely to have different ideas on our own. Different people almost guarantee different ideas. Creative also means practical. Practical always involves identifying and solving potential problems in the application of ideas. When we are the parent of an idea, it is easy to see only its strengths. Other people who do not feel the same sense of parental protectiveness add value to our process by being better able to see practical problems, that when solved, increase the success potentials and sustainability of our ideas.

From this perspective, we can expect more creativity—more and ultimately better ideas—from collaborative group efforts than from isolated individual efforts. If we want mediocrity, we only need to keep our thinking within the box of our own ideas and perspectives.

28 WE ARE SMARTER TOGETHER THAN WE ARE APART

Cooperation researcher Alfie Kohn tells that in a survey of 122 studies of people in North American corporations between the 1920's and 1980's, 90% indicated that cooperation promoted higher achievement in performance than individual or competitive work. Not only is individual and collective performance greater, job satisfaction increases as well. As Kohn puts it, "Those who work with, rather against others feel more in control of their own lives." This sense of control provides us with the basis for what Ed Deming referred to as joy and pride in work.

In the 1995 Harvard study of Inventor's Hall of fame inductees, we find that the reports by these inventors "explodes the myth that 'true genius is lone genius.'" Many indicated that without ongoing collaboration with chemists, engineers, managers, and sales people, their innovations would have never made it past the initial idea phase.

R&D manager, Mosongo Moukwa, describes his experience. "A team that works together is able to cover more ground and come out with a larger number of great ideas in a given time than a noncooperative group."

Forrest Bird, inventor of the respirator, relies heavily on collaboration in his creativity as an inventor. Clearly reflecting the quantum perspective, he says, "We're all a team in life, especially in innovation." Inventors and innovators today cannot imagine inventions coming from individual efforts.

Apparently it pays off. The Life Insurance division of American Express has become obsessed with bashing boundaries and barriers between people inside and outside the organization. As a result, profits have increased by 700%. No small change. One senior member tells us that with the company's obsession with teamwork, "The difference now is that I'm a part of the group...I enjoy it immensely."

Doug Hall and his band of merry advertising innovators known as Richard Saunders International boast about having at least 18 of their products in the average American home. Doug's spin on the secret to their success: "Everything I do involves a team effort."

Team effort has been dramatically and successfully represented by the Chicago Bulls over the past several seasons. Making this happen with a team of talented egos is no small task for coach-philosopher Phil Jackson. But he brings a clear quantum understanding of what makes for success on and off the court. He says, "A great player can't do it alone...five individuals can't beat a team that's dedicated to working together."

29 MIND-SIZE & HAT-SIZE

Many things in life can be measured. We can measure the size of our feet for shoes, waist for belts, and head for hat. One thing we can't measure is the size of our mind. Our mind is capable of thinking the thoughts of someone two thousand years ago, or the thoughts of someone two thousand miles away. We can have thoughts today that can be thought by people two or a hundred years from now.

A group of two or two hundred can literally "grow" an idea in the group's "mind." Mind is shared space. The more we invite people into our thinking process—inviting them to critique, enjoy, and modify our ideas—the more unlimited our mind becomes. Only a boundless mind can solve life's most "unsolvable" puzzles.

30 FAMOUS COLLABORATIONS

We have learned to have a romantic, though not necessarily accurate, notion about artists, inventors, and innovators. We think of them as lone wolves, working in self-obsessed little worlds until they are discovered for their isolated genius.

Consider a few famous collaborations. In each case, each partner admits to a productive interdependency without which they possibly could not have achieved what they did.

- Artists Picasso & Braque
- Physicists Heisenberg & Bohr
- Poets Pound & Eliot

- Composers Gilbert & Sullivan
- Comedy geniuses Bob & Ray
- Aviation pioneers the Wright Brothers
- Apple Computer founders Jobs & Wozniak
- Ice cream moguls Ben & Jerry
- Democracy developers Franklin & Jefferson
- Music innovators Lennon & McCartney

Dan Burrus again: "The most gifted creators are constantly exchanging information and ideas with others." Inventor Raymond Kurzweil agrees, "Inventing today is very much a team effort."

The great American writer Henry Miller spent the latter part of his career doing more painting than writing and often did group paintings, sharing the tasks of design, composition, specialization, and improvements. Even what traditionally has been treated as individual tasks can easily become collaborations. No one knows this better than American Greeting artists who labor together to bring us words for occasions that leave us struggling.

- Sony's CD players
- Apple's PC's
- NASA's developmental projects,
- Texas Instruments' pocket calculators
- Bell Lab's commercial communications satellites
- Ampex Corporation's VCR's

What do these have in common? They are all the result of inventive collaborations. Every one is a team effort.

31 A Collaboration To-Do List

1. The next time you get an idea that seems worthy of more thought, research, refinement or improvement, get other people involved. Let them share in the process of cultivating, growing, protecting this living idea you have been fortunate to discover.

2. Turn ideas into projects. Create an action plan with tasks defining what you'll need to do to take this idea to its next steps. Get other people involved in some or all of the tasks. Don't be shy—ask. Commit it to paper/disc and put a schedule on it—even if you have to revise your plan and schedule every week.

3. Disregard boundaries. So what if you need help on an idea from people at different levels or departments in the organization? Or for that matter, so what if they are in your vendor or customer organizations—or even competitor organizations?

4. Network like crazy. Even mildly obsessive networkers know that an idea, insight or connection can come from anywhere, anytime. The bigger your net, the more likely you are to get the answers, the questions or the help you need to get an idea moving. Remember the 6 degrees of connection: There are only about 6 people between you and every other human being on the planet. With the Internet, it's probably down to 3 or 4 by now. This is a global village.

5. Be very generous with credit. Give people credit for any help they give you. Do it publicly and privately—whichever makes the most political sense for you and them.

32 Two Tips On Teams

When you're part of a team dedicated to the creative process, there are two design considerations that can have a potentially important impact on the process and outcomes.

1 *Small is smart.*

Collaborative creativity teams do best when their size, scope and schedule is small. Participation is optimal when team size stays around 4-7 people. With fewer, you don't get enough of the kind of stimulation and diversity that helps make ideas unique and practical. With more, the group polarizes into those who dominate and those who disappear.

Innovators find that the narrower the focus, the easier it is to be inventive. Stay away from project scopes the size of "peace on earth" or "improving communication throughout the company." The more focused and measurable the scope, the more likely the team will be productive, efficient, and innovative.

It is important to set end-dates on any kind of innovative project. Otherwise you create multigenerational projects where the grandchildren of original members see the final phases of the project through. Project managers know well that the longer the project, the more chances there are for things to go wrong and get delayed. Nothing is more rewarding than getting a project done in a reasonably short time frame.

2 *Membership Counts.*

It matters whom you invite to participate on teams. There needs to be a good mix of knowledge and know-how related to the project focus. It is a good idea to always invite people who are expected to be end-users of the project's deliverables. End-users can bring fresh perspectives that elude experts. While you're at it, make sure you involve any decision-makers. The more they share in the process, the more they will feel protective and supportive of the outcomes.

Remember the rule "small is smart." If you have the interest and ability to get a larger number of people involved, divide the group into subgroups assigned to different phases or specific tasks within the project.

An interesting and effective way to limit the team is to create two levels of involvement called a Core Group and a Buy-In Group.

The Core Group is responsible for moving the project along. They attend meetings and do assignments related to the project. The Buy-In Group is a group of stakeholders who are each assigned to Core Group members. Throughout the entire project, Core Group members informally solicit input, ideas, and feedback from their assigned Buy-In Group members and represent those contributions in all Core Group discussions.

Except for project kickoff and closeout meetings, the Buy-In Group members are not obligated to scheduled formal meetings. This makes it easier to involve as many people as you'd like in the Buy-In Group without affecting the integrity of the Core Group's interactions. It also becomes a useful tool for involving people in the project who may be too busy (or obnoxious/intimidated/intimidating) to invite to meetings.

33 THE POLITICS OF CREATIVITY

In politically polarized environments, people are divided into sides dedicated to competing for what are believed to be limited resources. Everyone belongs to an "us" that implies a "them."

Political divisions prevent creativity because they prevent the kind of collaboration required to meet the requirements of many creative opportunities. You can reduce and eliminate these divisions by inviting "them" to join you in your creative process. Nothing builds sustainable bridges like creating together. The diversity will even make your ideas stronger than they would be otherwise. Without "them", many of our most creative ideas have absolutely no chance of becoming reality. With "them," more becomes more possible.

Practice no respect for boundaries that act as barriers to collaborative creativity. Be the one who suggests collaboration no matter how scary. There will always be more risks in not inviting a shared creative process than there ever are when we divide ourselves into two separate processes. There is no more dramatic evidence than in political environments that we are smarter together than apart.

Practicing Creativity

34 What's The Problem?

The most vibrant creative processes begin with questions.

A few years ago, a cross-functional team in a hospital worked on a project to improve the turnaround time on lab orders. The team started out with nine days of training in problem-solving. They learned a lot, except how to define problems in a creative way.

Dozens of unproductive meetings later and well before they were ready to present their deliverables, the team was asked to close out the project. Frustrated yet persistent, they decided to give it another chance. Just-in-time training gave them some new questions to start asking themselves—like, "What is this project's measurable deliverables?" This one question sparked a series of conversations and, within a short time, the project was successfully completed. Inventors all over the world tell us that if you're having a devil of a time solving the problem, you may not be starting off with the right questions (or any questions) in the first place.

In the beginning of many problem-solving projects that require fresh, creative thinking, the most important questions have to do with the definition of the problem. According to

Tom Logsdon "The way we state a problem can have a crucial impact on the way we attempt to solve it."

In a creative process, problems, projects, and opportunities are often posed as questions. How can we improve sales, speed or satisfaction? How can we come up with a better way to do this? What would give us better results here? Is there a way to make this more affordable? What would make people look at this and think, "Wow!"?

Creativity researchers Ray & Myers put it this way: "Implicitly or explicitly, creativity always begins with a question...The quality of your creativity is determined by the quality of your questions."

Although being creative can begin with a single question, don't assume that one question will be enough. Work from as many as possible. Some results have multiple requirements, so don't restrict yourself to just one or two questions.

Psychologist D. Noone suggests that in creativity, "The key is to have a lot of ideas, and the way to generate a lot of ideas is to have a lot of questions." In fact, the only way to get a lot of new answers to a problem or conflict is to start with a lot of new questions. Inventors and artists don't invent solutions as much as they invent questions that lead to solutions.

Not all questions are productive. There's no way to tell though, until you go where they lead. Some lead you to goldmines of ideas, hints, and directions. Others will lead you in circles.

If your questions aren't getting you to fresh, practical thinking, always look at your questions. As *Awaken The Giant Within* author Tony Robbins suggests, "If you want to change your reality, change your focus. If you want to change your focus, change the questions you're asking yourself." If you want solutions that no one else has, start asking questions that no one else is asking.

This process of asking new questions was a part of all great breakthroughs. For example, Velcro, inspired by the technology of field burrs, was the logical answer to a new question about how nature makes temporary fasteners.

Every day, consultants sit with problem-solving teams in companies and help get the job done. In more cases than not, the value added by consultants are the fresh sets of questions they bring to the table. Sometimes the most naive questions pack the most power to unleash the group's imaginations and capacity for consensus.

Ray & Myers tell us that in their experience with hundreds of executives in Fortune 500 and hot growth companies, even "Dumb questions lead you deeper into reality, truth and purpose. They inspire and expand you in some significant way."

Questions are tools that have the power to transform a circular meeting into a focused and productive one. The difference between a high performance group and the group from hell is not in their levels of education or motivation. As Tony Robbins says, "The only difference between people is the questions they ask."

35 12 ACTIVITIES TO EXPAND YOUR CREATIVE POTENTIALS

Once the problem is well-defined, it's time to get busy being creative. Here are 12 activities individuals and groups can use to develop their creativity potentials together. They are clustered together according to the creativity competency they best support.

The more you practice any of these activities, the more creative you will be, no matter how mundane or dramatic the challenge.

Tools for being open-minded
Curiosity
Multiple Uses
Upsides & Downsides

Tools for being inventive
Features & Benefits
Analogies
Variations & Alternatives

Tools for being provocative
Random Words
Ideal States
Rule Breaking

Tools for being practical
Secondary Problems
Idea Assessment
Action-Planning

---

36 TOOLS FOR BEING OPEN-MINDED

Curiosity

Think of as many questions about a situation as you can.

Take recent events in your organization, in your industry, or in any industry or market that impacts yours. Recent sales have skyrocketed. Your company lost/gained an important account. Trends indicate a growing reluctance by employees to relocate in their work. After lower prices on products, customer complaints start to increase.

Pick an event or trend that is interesting, intriguing, puzzling or contrary to common sense. Then start a list of questions. What about the trend or event are you curious about? If it was a problem you had to solve or something you'd have to explain, what questions would drive your research? If you could interview people who had already collected information about it, what would you ask them? Get the list as long as you can.

If your sales are down in a certain area, questions you raise might include:

- Have sales even been down before?
- Has the quality of the deliverables been different?
- Has something changed about buyers' interest or needs?
- Are sales up somewhere else?
- Are similar suppliers experiencing the same trend?
- Is there some change in the deliverable that would turn buyers toward more sales?
- Are there problems we haven't been aware of?

Practicing your curiosity leads to greater creativity because the creative process begins and ends with questions. Open-mindedness about anything begins with curiosity. In this Age of Information, questions expand the very "stuff" of the creative process.

Practice curiosity in everyday conversations and meetings. Be the one who keeps asking questions. The questions you're more likely to regret are not the ones you ask but the ones you don't ask. Different questions often lead to different insights. Your inventive spirit thrives in an environment of accumulating Ah-Ha's.

Multiple Uses

Think of as many uses for something as you can

Take any common object or product. A paper cup, straw, balloon, paper clip, abandoned landmark or discarded car tire. Go far beyond obvious uses as you can and make the list as long as you can. Be imaginative.

A paper cup can be used for protecting your ears at a very cold football game, catching bugs, holding worms for fishing bait or dipping in paint and making designs to decorate a wall or paper for gift wrapping.

One way to grow your list is by doing things to your object in ways that increase its potential uses. Distort, reshape, disassemble or coat your object. Wax a paper cup and insert a candle for a luminary to float on a pond. Tear your cup into shreds for packaging materials. Poke holes into it and use it as a sieve to drain pasta.

When the innovators at 3M put defective glue to use as a temporary adhesive to paper, they built a multi-million dollar business out of Post It Notes. Many inventions and art pieces simple create novel uses for things taken for granted or thrown away by uncreative people as "useless." Usefulness and uselessness is a matter of imagination. One person's garbage literally can become another's roses. Open-mindedness sees the infinite potential in even the most finite thing.

Upsides & Downsides

Think of possible advantages and disadvantages of something.

Take anything that could be the focus of controversy, debate or conflict for people in your organization, or anywhere in your world. Think of things that might easily polarize a group into two or three factions.

For example, a few years ago, an environmentalist group was polarized into two sides of a debate on whether to accept a large cash donation from a company with a history of what this group defined as less than ideal environmental practices.

The group only achieved consensus when they started to take an open-minded approach to the issue together. This meant looking at both sides.

Take one of your own examples and see how long you can get both sides of your lists. Include anything, and focus both on the short term as well as the long term. When you practice open-mindedness like this as a group, it become less likely that the group will polarize into a conflict, hard feelings, circular discussion and delayed decisions. With open-mindedness, we are all seeing the whole picture together. This is an excellent exercise to do as a group with any idea that starts to divide a group. Open-mindedness, when practiced together, brings us together.

General Electric leader Jack Welch tells his managers that the more we can agree on the problem, the faster we'll all come to similar conclusions on the solutions.

37 TOOLS FOR BEING INVENTIVE

Features & Benefits

Think of potential features and benefits of something.

Take any multifaceted product or part of a product and create two lists. List all of its features—anything you expect it to include. List all of its benefits—anything value users might expect to get from it.

The features of car dashboards, for example, include things like glove compartments, steering wheels, radios and tape or CD players, instrumentation and gages, cup holders, and so on. Benefits include safety, car maintenance, convenience, storage, and entertainment.

Being able take inventory of the ingredient elements and the potential benefits to something is vitally important to the creative process, especially when it is collaborative. We grow a fresh set of alternatives and variations to ideas by changing some of the elements, or thinking of other ways to provide the same benefits. It begins with this basic ability to appreciate the components and advantages of ideas.

In a group, nothing is more important than seeing the benefits of people's ideas. Every idea, even if it has a dozen serious downsides, always has some benefit. When we can take that benefit and find other ways to achieve it, we have ecologically used the initial idea as a very valuable springboard to new and perhaps better ideas.

Once you've identified all of the benefits and features, you can reinvent and rearrange them to create new possibilities.

Analogies

Think of things that have similar features and benefits.

You can start with your focus from the *Features & Benefits* activity. What else in your world has similar features and benefits?

For the dashboard, suitcases also have compartments for storage, as do cabinets with drawers, golf bags, and attic trunks. Instrument panels also occur on microwaves and automatic tooling equipment. On the benefit side, other forms of entertainment include VCRs and professional story tellers.

In the creative process, this list of analogies leads us to new inventive possibilities. Maybe when you buy a car, you can sign up for a service that provides you with a professional story teller who can accompany you and your children on long trips. Maybe small VCR screens can be installed on the back of front seats for rear seat passengers, making long trips shorter. Maybe there should be drawer options on dashboards, or minimicrowave ovens for heating cold coffee or popping pop corn when you're traveling.

Analogies lead us to fresh thinking, some of which may need to evolve into more practical applications, and some of which may be immediately implementable.

Variations & Alternatives

Think of different versions of or approaches to an idea.

When you start a list of ideas and feel the list running dry, go back to some of your original ideas and start developing variations and alternatives to them.

You have an idea to send people out to training for skills they need in their work. What other kinds of training might be possible? Maybe people can get a series of tapes for their commutes that they can listen to and get training from that. Maybe they can take home video tapes to put into their VCRs. Maybe they can be trained by a noncompetitive organization already doing the training in-house for their people. Think of as many variations on the original ideas as possible.

Alternatives are different approaches to the same objective. In a large retirement community, many residential buildings were joined by miles of concrete sidewalks. Every winter, snow crews would have to salt the sidewalks often to keep them in good condition for the residents who had a wide range of physical mobility. Every year, salt would destroy the grass along-side the walkways and the grass would have to be replaced.

After several suggestions, one alternative caught the group's attention, interest, and approval. Instead of replacing the grass with grass, replace it with rocks. The idea was to have a rock garden day in which residents, staff, and the community were invited to bring and place small attractive rocks alongside the walkways, resulting in both an esthetic improvement as well as a safe, cost-effective place for salt every winter.

38 TOOLS FOR BEING PROVOCATIVE

Random Words

Think of alternatives and variations sparked by random words.

An outpatient surgery division of an HMO is looking for ideas to increase its business. It starts with a random word: umbrella. The idea here is to think of associations to our random word. In this case we might think of how umbrellas protect us, how they are portable and easy to open and close and are designed with spokes coming out from a center point. We may think of umbrellas used by mimes doing high wire acts.

Taking the idea of opening and closing easily, portability, and the pattern of spokes, we might think about how a surgery center might move out from a central point and be easy to open with the possibility of portability. Maybe we could arrange with companies using the HMO to schedule mobile surgery units that can visit companies to provide certain kinds of outpatient procedures for employees and their families.

A team of people from sales, marketing, and engineering are convened to come up with ideas to increase sales. They also use umbrella and decide to focus on its protection benefit. Someone raises the question, "Why would we need to protect our product?" The question leads to the idea that other suppliers are always coming out with competitive models capturing sales with improved features.

Maybe we could design parts of our products to be easily interchangeable with updated versions featuring technical, esthetic, and user-friendly features. Maybe as these are developed, instead of being tempted to go out and buy a competitor's improved model, customers with our products can go to a store or make a call for delivery of these replacement modules that continuously update the functions and features of the product.

With on-line airline ticket services, we now have access to much of the information travel agents had. We can now shop rates and availability, book our own flights including seat assignments and make cancellations. This creates a problem for travel agents.

We can start with the word frog. Frogs can live in two different environments, water and land. They change forms in their development and can move easily from one environment to the other. Maybe travel agents can become part-time human resource staff in companies where travel is common. As subcontractors they can operate their own travel business half-time and the other half-time work as employees in human resource functions. This gives them cross-visibility and accessibility for both functions. Other employees can use their services to arrange both business and personal travel arrangements. Everyone wins.

Random words work by getting our thinking out of their usual patterns. Any words can provide the magic for the process. Open a dictionary, catalog or newspaper; pick out a word and you have an instant spark to ignite your imagination.

Ideal States

Think of ways to eliminate the problems that have to be solved.

Every company provides training—job training, management training, training on new equipment (hardware) and software. Instead of thinking about how to improve training, we think about ways to possibly eliminate training.

Maybe we could improve our recruitment process so that people hired need little or no training. Maybe we could design jobs in a way that minimizes the need for new skills. Maybe equipment and software can be better designed to limit the need for any training.

Here we're looking for the ideal situation related to our innovative focus. A group of employees in an auto plant recently were working on a better way to design the refueling functions in cars. The idea was to reduce the inconvenience of wrestling with pumps and hoses. From an ideal states perspective, the group started working on how to eliminate the need for getting out of the car altogether. This creativity led to ideas of automated fuel cartridge replacements from under the car at gas stations. Who knows where else it may lead?

Rule-Breaking

Think of ways that breaking rules can lead to new ideas.

Rules are expectations about the way things work. Rule: We need traffic lights, especially at the busiest intersections. Rule breaking here might begin with the provocation, "Busiest intersections have no traffic lights."

Maybe all cars have visual or sound signals activated at intersections. Maybe you can choose your own musical or graphic signals activated from your dashboard or projected into your windshield. There can be brightly lighted strips in the road that signal traffic patterns. Maybe some busy intersections are designed with underpasses.

Recently in New York city, city officials and taxi companies worked on a two problems that have been around for years. Airport roadways are jammed with taxis sitting and waiting for traveler's' business. Besides being a problem for people trying to maneuver through airports, it leaves fewer taxis for people in the city needing short rides.

One idea is to invent ways to increase city taxi traffic for those stranded for their short trips. One logical expectation might be to lower fares for short trip customers, so more request taxis more frequently. Breaking this rule, we get the idea: Raise fares for short trips. This idea was one that actually caught more than a few people's support. If fares go up for short trips, this would give airport taxi-potatoes incentives to stay in the city, easing airport traffic congestion and satisfying more short trip customers.

When you're creating provocations, remember Edward de Bono's inspiring upside down airplane.

39 TOOLS FOR BEING PRACTICAL

Secondary Problems

Think of problems created by ideas and solutions for them.

In an idea session at a manufacturing company, an idea comes up in a group. Maybe we could start producing containers for our line of liquid products that are currently purchased from external suppliers. This is a solution designed to decrease container costs, improve their quality, and strengthen just-in-time delivery capabilities.

Like any solution, there are secondary problems, that when solved, make the idea practical—sellable, affordable, implementable.

- We have never shopped for the raw materials that go into these containers
- We don't have the experience making these kinds of containers
- We would have to shift money from somewhere to build this new business unit
- We don't have extra people for this new function
- We don't currently have space for it

The list can be long or short. The key is to do whatever needs to be done to go after these secondary problems one by one. With enough collaborative creativity, even the most "impossible" become solvable. This can include cooking up more ideas, or doing some research that can answer some of the questions implied by the problems that need practical solutions. The more secondary problems we solve, the more practical our ideas become.

Is your group having a problem with the idea of mini-microwaves in the minivan dash? How about if they only work when the minivan is stationary.

Bottom line: Always expect some secondary problems in even your most attractive and "simple" ideas. Look at secondary problems simply as opportunities to evolve good ideas into great ones. Value people who point out secondary problems to even our favorite ideas. Never give up. The difference between possible and impossible, can and can't is only a matter of imagination.

Idea Assessment

Think of benefits we could use to assess and compare ideas.

Sometimes you have a long list of ideas. When they get their creative energies flowing, groups can come up with literally dozens of ideas. Sometimes the task is to filter out those with the least potentials for success, leaving you with only the best.

A company wants to improve its compensation system—what people get beyond their base pay for achieving specific goals, targets or improvements. They're looking at 8 different models and want to implement the best.

Create a list of benefits you would want to see delivered by the "ideal" model.

- Everyone perceives it as fair and non-biasing
- It's compatible with company profit requirements
- It rewards both individual and team efforts
- It doesn't punish people with conditions outside their control
- It is easy to administrate
- It is easy to explain and understand

Once you have this list, compare each model against each criterion. Use a scale of 1-5. How well do we think each model will be able to deliver each benefit? When you add the scores (and adjust them on a weighting scale if you want), you have an instantly-prioritized list of ideas from those with the greatest to least success potential.

The more specific, measurable, accurate, and complete your list of benefit requirements, the more effective the process.

Action-Planning

Think of all the steps involved in implementing an idea.

An organization wants to set up a new office. This is the highest scoring idea from an idea assessment session. What needs to be done to make this happen?

Start a list of all possible tasks you think will be required to achieve the deliverable, a new office opened. As you begin, don't waste time trying to work on sequencing and identifying tasks—just identify them.

- Select a location
- Decide on lease or build
- Develop a media package
- Establish an opening date
- Arrange an openhouse event
- Order new equipment
- Select staff
- Train staff
- Set up network links
- Decide on parameters for differences from other locations

Once your list seems complete, sequence the ideas. If you put each task on a Post It Note, arrange each visually on a wall, showing sequential and simultaneous task relationships. This positions you to then identify assignments and end-dates for each task so the solution has successful implementation.

Ideas are only creative if they're useful, practical, destined for effective and efficient implementation. Every new idea typically requires more than a few minutes of action planning. In a group, everything matters—getting tasks identified, sequenced, assigned and planned. As every project manager knows from experience, the secret to performance is in the planning.

40 More Ideas Lead To Better Ideas

Watch a group not particularly known for being creative. Everyone takes turns proposing their first idea as "the one" that's going to do the trick. People hope to begin with the last idea they'll need. They strive to *have* ideas when in many cases, they would be more productive striving to *develop* ideas. They end up with short lists of ideas that don't particularly inspire consensus or decisive action.

Creative groups do the opposite. Practicing idea detachment, they aim at growing their lists as long as they can. They have learned that in the creative process, quantity leads to quality. Creativity expert Stephen Grossman makes the observation that "Breakthrough ideas (if they surface at all) dependably appear in the later stages of the brainstorming process." Nobel Laureate Linus Pauling puts it simply: "The best way to have good ideas is to have lots of ideas."

Reinventing and reengineering, look at your first few ideas lightly. Treat them as sketches you come back to later, in the meantime create whole different approaches to the problem or question you're working on. Let first ideas evolve into the next.

Beethoven once described his creative process like this: "I change many things, discard others, and then try again and again until I am satisfied." In other words, plan on every creative process being messy and evolutionary.

41 WHAT DO YOU THINK.... IDEAS GROW ON TREES?

In an Inc Magazine poll of CEO's, the two most frequently named sources for new ideas were:

1. Magazines
2. Customers.

Mystery writer Agatha Cristie found many of her best ideas popping out among soap bubbles while washing dishes. Playwright Sam Shepard does his best writing while driving. Hemingway found his muses at tables in cafes. At Ames NASA base, index cards and pens are available in toilet stalls.

Creativity writer and author of *What A Great Idea!*, Chic Thompson gives us an interesting list of the 10 top idea-inspiring venues.

10. Manual labor
9. Listening to sermons
8. At midnight
7. Exercising
6. Doing light reading
5. Waking up in boring meetings
4. Going to sleep & waking up at night
3. Commuting
2. In the shower
1. On the toilet

Add to this, other possibilities: Internet bulletin board browsing, taking classes inside or outside your field and visiting museums, galleries and trade shows.

A great way to unleash your wisdom is through wit. According to humor expert Joel Goodman, there is a clear relationship between humor and creativity. The Ha-Ha leads us to the Ah-Ha. We can stimulate our creative energies with an hour of comedy favorites—from classics to contemporary. Rent comedy videos, take a few friends to a comedy club or do some reading from the humor section of your bookstore. Don't be surprised if you find your Ah-Ha's coming more often thanks to a few Ha-Ha's.

If some preschoolers ask you where ideas come from, spend a couple of hours with them in their tree house. What you're both likely to find is that ideas can indeed grow on trees.

Designing Meetings

42 The Ingredients Of Successful Meetings

In the process of collaborative creativity, meetings are opportunities for conversations where we together practice being open-minded, inventive, provocative, and practical. A meeting can be formally scheduled or spontaneous, lasting a few minutes or a few hours, involving just two or twenty people. It can have a detailed agenda or only the spark of a question, update or proposal. They can happen anywhere (or "everywhere", if electronically).

In the world of performance, design is everything. This is particularly true about meetings. Whether they involve two or twenty of us over a few minutes or few hours, the structure of our process together determines the quality and satisfaction that comes out of it.

Obvious or not, all meetings have structure. As we know from chaos theory, we can always see structure in chaos if we look close and long enough. The only thing nature knows how to do is to happen in patterns.

Here are a few ingredients that can make meetings successful when collaborative creativity is the objective.

1. Agendas with timeframes

Successful agendas identify the deliverables expected at the end of a discussion, presentation or brainstorming process. This is in contrast to agenda items that only describe the focus. An agenda item described as "*Personnel changes*" is a focus, not a deliverable. It defines what will be discussed, but not what we'll have at the end of the discussion. If you allow groups to know the focus but not the deliverable, they may never get to closure.

Tell people in a group what the deliverable is and watch them get to it. With "*Personnel changes*", the expected outcome may be an action plan outlining how changes will be implemented.

It is sometimes useful to set a timeframe for each agenda item and keep people to it. If they finish early, move on. If work goes over, you have three options:

- Have the group decide if it wants to redistribute more time to it by taking time from later agenda items

- Have the group form a subgroup to take the work off-line and return to the next meeting with results

- Have the group decide on a completion date for any deferred work.

Whether you strictly hold the group to timeframes or not, even loose and flexible timeframes have the tendency to keep the pace productive, minimize tangents, and encourage efficiency.

2. Balance of play & seriousness

We have inherited an unfortunate legacy of belief in seriousness as a requirement for productive work. "Stop fooling around and get back to work" represents an unquestioned misunderstanding of work, especially work in meetings aimed at creative outcomes. In the worst cases we become, as one engineering project manager puts it, "serious about our seriousness."

Be careful not to set a tone that inhibits humor, good-hearted teasing, wild tangents, giggling side conversations, and general fun. In the spirit of provocation, the least-related idea can spark the most creative possibilities. There is perhaps nothing more uncreative or unproductive than a group obsessed with seriousness that would make a congregation of Puritans weep.

The Tao of meetings is balance. Let discussions get serious and debate spirited. Let them be playful and light. In either case, it often takes little to lighten up an overly stiff atmosphere with some humor. It takes just as little to bring chaos back to the task at hand. Groups appreciate neither extreme. Practice the middle way. In research on the role of humor in problem-solving, marriage partners and therapists overwhelmingly agree on the relationship between playfulness and creativity in collaborative relationships.

3. Differences are welcome and even valued

The collision of differences is inevitable in collaborations—especially when people aren't used to working together or when they represent different functions. Encourage everyone to look at different facts, perceptions, interpretations, speculations, and suggestions as potentially value-added.

This is particularly important when a group polarizes around two options, as if they were trying out for a "Tastes-great, less-filling" commercial. Always work from the "more ideas lead to better ideas" guideline. Get the group as far beyond dueling ideas as it can. If everyone has to go off and do more thinking, research or both, have them do it.

Groups find it useful to create a groundrule that everyone must say something positive about an idea before they introduce a concern, question or problem with it.

4. Every agenda is treated as "ours"

Meetings are successful when people work as partners to address every agenda item. There is absolutely no room for "Not-our-problem" perspectives. When we work within any living system—such as a group—any part's gain ultimately becomes every part's gain. We have everything to gain by *sharing* responsibility for problems and opportunities.

We tend to be much smarter, more agile, and creative when we work together rather than apart.

5. Comments and questions about the process are encouraged

There is power in talking about what happens in a meeting as it happens. Groups that spend a few minutes at the end of meetings to lightly "process" the meeting's productivity and satisfaction tend to become more productive and collaborative in future meetings.

When meetings bog down, use questions to get people talking about the process.

- *What are we trying to accomplish here?*
- *Does anyone have any suggestions on how we should approach this agenda item?*
- *Who can summarize what we've agreed on so far?*
- *What's the deliverable from this discussion?*
- *Since we're low on time for this, how should we get closure on it?*
- *Can we take a quick vote and see how much consensus we have so far?*

In productive meetings, people talk about how they will approach an agenda item before they get into it. They might decide for example, whether the item requires a list, decision, the development of a plan or some idea assessment.

A hallmark of unproductive groups is an obsession with content, to the exclusion of talking together about the direction, sequencing and timing of the process. In contrast, productive groups punctuate conversations with what communication experts call "meta-talk"—talking about our process of talking.

Efficient and effective groups, when overwhelmed with the complexity, size or sensitivity of an issue first talk about how to approach the issue before getting into it. The group moves in a direction that has been defined by consensus. Their meetings become a productive flow from one thinking task to another.

Common thinking tasks that productive groups select in designing or course-correcting their process include:

- Developing a list of questions to be addressed (unknowns to be researched or clarified)
- Developing a list of strategies to consider
- Ranking, rating or voting on listed items in order to narrow down the list
- Creating scheduled assignments for strategies selected
- Forming subgroups to achieve work for the group between meetings
- Getting status reports on the progress of projects, tasks and assignments
- Clearing the air of questions, concerns or misunderstandings.

43 WHERE DO YOU GET THE TIME?

When there is pressure to produce, there is temptation to treat meetings as an interruption to "work." This is a barrier to collaborative creativity, grounded in a basic misunderstanding of productivity.

Productivity improves because we have cooked up ideas on how to do things faster, better, cheaper or easier. Productivity does not efficiently improve simply by trying to get more people doing more of the same. No new productivity standards are met without new ideas on how to make these happen. Thinking has always been and will continue to be the most important part of work. Because most productivity challenges involve more than one function, solutions require meetings of the minds.

Make a practice of referring to meetings as "work." Have more working meetings and leave updating to networked PC's.

"Where are we going to get time to meet?" is perhaps the wrong question. The right question: "Where are we going to get the time to handle problems if we don't meet and come up with some fresh and practical approaches?" If we have time for anything, it is because we create it for that purpose. No dimension of work is more important than the thinking required for it.

Creativity happens in a series of insights that happen in instants. Many creative moments take no time at all.

44 COLLABORATION TECHNOLOGY

In collaborative creativity, we strive to work as a single mind, sharing opportunity, information, and ideas. Together we bring seed ideas through their evolution to consensus and ultimately to results.

"To get a communal mind going, you want to get people's minds to interact as components of a larger mind," says MIT researcher-writer Michael Shrage. Ideas are the content of mind; mind is the context. Essentially, mind is the space where ideas emerge and evolve. Shared mind is shared space. From his work with corporations he suggests that "All collaborations rely on shared space. It may be a blackboard, a napkin, a piano keyboard, a rehearsal room, a prototype or a model."

Shared space is a space where ideas can be seen, heard, touched, felt, shaped, and reshaped. Post It Notes are a handy tool for creating shared space. As people have ideas, they can post them, arrange them relationally according to category, schedule or responsibility.

Flipcharts with newsprint, 3M's Post It Note newsprint paper, electronic writing boards and good old white boards are all useful technologies. Some of the best art sketched by teams of artists in studios today are simply chalked out on concrete floors or crayoned on papered walls.

One of the hottest examples of innovations in meeting management is the array of software packages now available for electronic meetings. Here, several PC's are networked, sometimes in the same physical space. The software allows people to simultaneously enter, organize, comment on, rank, and vote on ideas. Everything entered shows up on everyone's screen, allowing for anyone to comment and participate in the development, refinement, and prioritization of ideas.

Electronic sessions have several benefits:

- Ideas and voting can show up anonymously or not— giving the group the option of unbiased responses
- Dozens of ideas can be recorded in the same time it would take to record just a few on newsprint
- Voting calculations are instant, resulting in both graphic and list displays of statistical trending within the group on each item listed
- Since everyone has their own PC, dominating and disappearing is minimized—leveling the participation playing field
- Deliverables are saved on disc for other groups to work on or for future sessions
- Everything can be immediately translated into hard copies for the group members to take into breakout sessions.

Electronic bulletin boards and real-time chatrooms on the wide range of Internet services provide even a larger potential shared space for collaborations.

45 THE POWER OF SHARED SPACE

In a control systems company a few years ago, a group of employees and managers was being trained as internal trainers. In a session on group facilitation, everyone was assigned the task of facilitating a simulated discussion. The objective was to optimize participation and keep the group focused. The directions prohibited any use of visual technology to record ideas.

Why this strange direction? Visual technology instantly creates a shared space and gets everyone literally thinking on the same page. The aim in this exercise was to have trainer recruits practice facilitating groups simply using their personal skills. In the end, trainers got an important lesson in the power of collaborative technology.

As Michael Shrage says, "To a real extent, the quality of technology determines the quality of our interactions."

This insight into shared thinking supports why locked suggestion boxes are the quickest way to prevent collaborative creativity. This is especially when there is an expectation that the box is connected to external incentives awarded to the individuals who get the best idea and get it there first.

Agrarian Age wisdom held that "a good craftsman never blames his tools." In the Information Age where tool technology has in many cases advanced beyond the technology shaped by the tools, tool designers live by the opposite paradigm. In the Information Age, it could be said that "good craftspeople always look for better ways to design their tools"—especially when tools include the information that in-forms both the process and content of our work.

46 NO ROOM FOR FEAR

There is no room for fear in collaborative creativity. Fear of speaking up, voicing illogical ideas or concerns dramatically limits a group's potentials for being open-minded, inventive, provocative and practical. All four competencies suffer when people hesitate to voice ideas, facts, questions, considerations, and alternatives.

Seattle-based organizational development consultants Kathleen Ryan and Daniel Oestreich have developed a list of actions that tend to shut down participation in meetings. Here is a sample of items on that list.

- Responding to ideas with silence
- Giving people "the look"
- Abruptness
- Insults & put-downs
- Blaming & threats
- "My ideas are obviously superior" attitudes

Each creates the kind of fear that encourages self-filtering of ideas and contributions to the process. If you're in a group that practices or allows these kinds of obstacles, suggest consensus on groundrules that discourage idea-limiting words or actions. In the collaborative process aimed at creativity, you cannot afford to miss out on even one person's contributions.

47 Two Tools For Consensus-Building

Consensus is not necessarily a required, but is often a desired and valuable objective in any collaborative process. Ideas that win a group's consensus have more success potential in the implementation phase than those that do not. Consensus can be built or artificially imposed (coerced consensus). While voting itself doesn't build consensus, it can be a very useful tool for testing the level of consensus in a group where the level of consensus is not altogether obvious.

With a few good tools, you can avoid the kind of voting on ideas that polarizes the group into winners and losers. In meetings aimed at collaborative creativity, the ideal is to design the process in a way that allows the group to naturally evolve ideas that lead to consensus.

There are dozens of tools that can help with this. Here are two very simple yet powerful tools—the *Knowns & Unknowns* and the *Idea Garden.*

1. Knowns & Unknowns

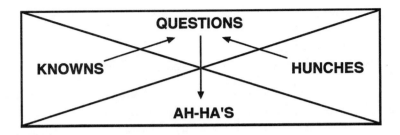

Consensus on solutions begins with consensus on the situation. Bring a group of people together for a creativity session—especially a diverse group of people from different functions—and from six people you may get eight different pictures of the opportunity on the table.

This is not bad. Diverse information makes for a richer—often more complete and accurate—understanding of the reality parameters and requirements that all new ideas must meet or exceed if they are to be useful.

There are two important objectives in the "problem understanding" phase of the creative process:

1. To get everyone working together to create a single common picture of "what is"

2. To expand and deepen the group's understanding of this picture.

The *Knowns & Unknowns* tool begins with the group identifying everything it knows for sure about the situation. This is a list of facts. Take a project of developing an advertising brochure for a new product or service. Some of the knowns might include:

- The specific services or products to be addressed
- Their specific features and benefits
- The copy audience demo/psychographics
- The costs of similar brochures developed in past projects

- The schedule expected on delivery
- Whether any other media for advertisement will be used with it (e.g. a home page on the World Wide Web)
- How brochures will be distributed

It is important to keep any speculations, educated guesses and assumptions off this list.

While this list is being completed, the group works at the same time on their list of unknowns. These can include any of the following:

- Things about the situation that for the group are assumptions, hunches or guesses at this point
- Things about the situation the group find's interesting, important to look into, confusing, or perplexing
- Things about the situation that need to be researched, clarified or decided.

A list of some unknowns might include:

- What graphics options can we consider?
- Are there cost parameters that have already been set?
- Are there other media that will be used to advertise these products/services at the same time (e.g. pages on a Web Site)?
- If so, what will they be?
- Are there special language considerations?
- What kind of image are we trying to project?
- Does the format have to compatible with any other formats?
- Are there printing specifications we have to meet?

It is important to record all hunches and questions. Translate all of the hunches into questions, assign people to questions and reconvene with the new knowns. The longer your list of questions, the more potential there is for unexpected insights and Ah-Ha's.

These are just a few of the many benefits from this process:

- Everyone gets to contribute (and feel valued for) their unique perspectives as the group weaves together the tapestry of picture-building
- The group moves from having several partial pictures to one complete shared picture
- Information gaps, instead of being barriers to the group's creativity, are instead leveraged as tools to expand possibilities when they are transformed into questions
- The group's intuition is leveraged as a vital tool for gaining important insights into reality factors and requirements

2. The Idea Garden

All living things represent the convergence of sun, water, air, and soil. Together, these elements allow seeds to move through every phase of development. Because ideas are living things, they too require fertile gardens in which to grow.

The *Idea Garden* brings together the essential elements necessary for growing a rich harvest of new ideas. The *Idea Garden* is the convergence of open-mindedness, inventiveness, provocation, and pragmatism required to grow ideas. It is a visual tool for stimulating, capturing, organizing, and developing the evolution of ideas in an idea session. In the *Idea Garden,* contributors are given four areas in which to generate ideas.

1. Broad Ideas (Air)

Here we're looking for any ideas that are vague, fuzzy, and unspecific, like "better communication", "more training" and "a better presence or image in our market." When ideas come up in a creativity session, they do not always come fully outlined with details. General ideas often sound more like outcomes and requirements than strategies. They are important to capture on paper/screen/board and kept visible as sparks to more specific ideas as the process evolves. In an idea session on orienting new people to their jobs, broad ideas might include peer buddy-systems, on-line help screens, and interactive videos.

2. Detailed Ideas (Sun)

Here we record every specific idea that comes up in the group's process. The more details the better; the more specific options the better. More details mean more practical ideas and a wider variety of ideas to draw from and use to build stronger consensus. It is important to record (plant) every idea and alternative generated by reshaping the details of ideas that have already been planted in the garden. In the training of new people, new people can be assigned to retired job experts contracted on a part-time basis. Training videos can feature local sports and media celebrities.

3. Considerations (Soil)

A practical group can see secondary problems with just about any idea. Some ideas will raise concerns, others will raise important and interesting questions. Foster this. Record everything that comes up in this section and encourage the use of considerations to craft a better, longer and richer list of general and specific options, alternatives, and variations. Treat everything as a potential spark for idea evolution. This section sometimes plays the vital role of garden compost, without which no living thing blossoms or bears fruit. Problems with the buddy-system can include the passing on of bad habits. Celebrities may not be available for training videos.

4. Variations (Water)

If people in the group can think of different variations on specific ideas that comes up, record them in this section. The goal is to grow this list as long as possible. When people "but" in ("yes, that's a good idea, but..."), encourage different variations on what has already been created. Especially encourage any that can solve problems and questions associated with any ideas generated. Buddy-system people can be selected from other companies who have the job competencies without the cultural baggage. Celebrity videos can feature advertisements of the celebrity organizations and favorite causes.

Make sure every single alternative and variation gets listed and stays visible. You never know when one will become a springboard into new possibilities. Especially encourage the development of ideas that can combine "the best of" several different options already listed. These often have the best potential for resolving conflicts and building consensus.

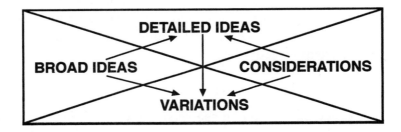

In the *Idea Garden*, the group is encouraged to work in all sections simultaneously. This is in sharp contrast to traditional "brainstorming" in which people are discouraged from working "creatively" and critically at the same time.

Talk to successful artists and inventors and you'll hear the same thing—a rule that is counterintuitive to what most of us have been taught to believe and practice in the brainstorming process. The rule in brainstorming has always been: separate the generation of ideas from the assessment of them. Who knows where this paradigm came from, but it is becoming more clear that it did not come from the actual creative and inventive processes of today's most successful and original artists and inventors.

Working to help his art students become more inventive, Claus Moje encourages his students to be continuously critical in their individual and shared creative processes. He sees the freedom to both imagine and critique as vital to the cultivation of creativity.

The magic in the *Idea Garden* is the sense of unrestricted freedom and synergy between the four basic creativity competencies that it brings to any group's creative process. It is a simple and powerful tool that, with use, gives us better results each time we use it. In classic brainstorming, criticism and tangents were always "forbidden fruit." By contrast, we regain our original sense of harmony with our creative nature because in the *Idea Garden*, there is no forbidden fruit and every temptation is encouraged.

48 THE FACILITATOR ROLE

Many groups prefer to work with a designated facilitator. If you have the privilege to play this role in a group, here are six important ways you can add value.

1. Information Sharing

Share with the group any kind of information that can help people be open-minded, inventive, provocative, and practical. If there are key parameters, requirements, and conditions that need to be met by any new ideas, help the group get clear on them at the front in the process.

2. Agenda-Building

Guide the group in determining the content and sequencing of agenda items, expected deliverables, and timeframes. This is particularly important at the end of a meeting to establish expectations for the next meeting.

3. Process Guide

Suggest the introduction and timing of the thinking task the group will share at each point in the process. When conversations unravel several ideas, summarize often. Move the group back from unproductive circles and tangents; move them on to the next task when one is completed. Suggest votes to test for levels of consensus when agreement needs to be clarified. If important information can only be gained by doing some kind of research or experimentation, prevent the group from wasting time trying to use discussion to answer their questions. Instead, get the group involved in whatever action research they'll need to get these questions answered.

4. Optimizing Participation

Ask questions that will get people thinking, talking, and generating information and ideas. Introduce tools and activities to get a large group into small, more productive groups. Call on people, pass out Post It Notes or establish ground rules if the group polarizes into those who dominate and those who disappear. Suggest the creation of sub-groups to do any work that doesn't necessarily require the whole group to do.

5. Facility Arrangements

Work with people to take care of rooms, equipment, meeting locations, layouts. Pay attention to details; environment can be a significant ingredient in the creative process. Use whatever resources you can to make environments interesting, convenient, comfortable and conducive of conversation and group interaction.

6. Participating Member

Add whatever you can to help the group stay open-minded, inventive, provocative, and practical. This includes any kind of information, ideas, questions, idea assessments concerns, process comments, suggestions, provocations, alternatives, and variations on ideas that can add value to the process and product. Be as generous as you expect everyone else to be. Don't worry about bringing in your own obsessions (AKA "vision"), opinions, and biases. Who knows? They may provoke exciting possibilities and breakthroughs. Facilitation is just another hat you wear while wearing the participant hat.

One of the most important tasks of a facilitator is keeping communication clear, open, and direct. As a facilitator listening to a group's interaction, always ask yourself: "Is everyone clear on what's being said or asked?" and "Is everyone being clear on what they're saying and asking?"

The facilitator's role is to make sure:

- Everything vague is defined
- Everything suggested has a response
- Everything questioned is answered
- Everything posed as a concern is addressed
- Everything deflected is scheduled to be addressed
- Everything debated and decided is summarized
- Everything decided is recorded.

In a group, creativity can only be shared when communication is high quality. When people don't necessarily speak and listen in the same language, it is (at least) the facilitator's job to get things translated quickly and accurately. In a group of people who are naturally creative on their own, the quality of communication together can be the biggest barrier or bridge to their creative potential together.

Do groups always need a facilitator? Not necessarily. The creative process requires comments and suggestions that facilitate creative dialogue. These can and should come from everyone. Productive groups tend to share rather than delegate this responsibility. The more a group develops its collaborative potentials for creativity, the more seamless (and powerful) this function becomes.

49 WHEN YOU'RE NOT "THE FACILITATOR"

You can add immeasurable value to collaborative creativity when you are not specifically designated "the facilitator." Facilitation is a way of being and participating in a group that helps the group become and stay open-minded, inventive, provocative, and practical together. A group's process can get rolling and roll over fragile insights and ideas that, if kept in the process by good facilitation, can add value to the quality of the group's process and outcome.

Even, and sometimes especially, when you're not the designated facilitator, do whatever you can to optimize participation and keep contributions from getting lost in the process. Suggest ideas, propose the preposterous, ask good questions, change your questions and ask better ones, suggest some research or bringing in a few more fresh perspectives. Help people feel as committed to the evolution of ideas as they would be to any plant, garden or child of theirs.

50 BIG MEETINGS: LESSON IN CREATIVE FLEXIBILITY

Meetings with large groups (50-250) can be interesting tools for stimulating fresh thinking and moving people toward consensus. Any size group can be divided into several small groups, each assigned with the same or different thinking tasks.

Post It Notes can be used to collect, display, and ultimately categorize a wide variety and large quantity of ideas from groups. Ideas can stay displayed in common areas over a specific time period so that people can add ideas whenever they can. Networked PC's with bulletin board and chat room capabilities can provide the same function, especially for people separated by one or more time zones.

Small groups can always be assigned to "harvest" ideas, removing redundancies, combining ideas into interesting "idea packages" and turning promising ideas into projects that take them all the way to implementation.

With a little imagination and a large appreciation for the generative power of facilitated chaos, any size, shape, or configuration of group can be used in any phase of any creative, inventive, or innovation process.

Winning Support

51 Is Resistance Inevitable?

Support from decision-makers and end-users is a often a practical requirement for idea success. While resistance in the process of idea development can add immeasurable value to the evolution of an idea, resistance ultimately keeps ideas from being taken seriously, being funded, or being implemented.

At any point in the process, resistance is not always inevitable. While new approaches can represent change, they do not necessarily cause resistance. The blanket statement that "people resist change" is an exaggeration of what can be the obvious byproduct of a practice of excluding the thinking of key stakeholders from the creative process. Getting resistance is most likely to the degree that we exclude stakeholders from the creative process.

Whether you like to work on new ideas with other people or not, collaborative creativity is more practical than individual creativity any time. Support from diverse groups is a requirement for idea success.

When change represents improvements that we had a hand in crafting, change is welcome. Look at the variety of complaints that come up in union grievances and climate surveys. Every one is a cry for change of one kind or another. The overriding theme: We want changes (improvements) in areas, and we're not seeing them come fast enough. Change is not a problem.

As indivisible parts of a universe where change is the only constant, change is our nature. We do not resist change; we resist being excluded from the process of changing. We tend to support what we help create.

52 ALTERNATIVES TO RESISTANCE

Until we participate in the development of an idea, it is most tempting to resist it. To resist is to treat an idea as lacking practical or provocative or informative value. In many cases, resistance is more a matter of perspective than substance.

- *"That'll never work"*
- *"I don't hear customers complaining about it"*
- *"We already tried that"*
- *"It's too complicated"*
- *"It's really good enough the way it is"*
- *"That's not our problem/job"*
- *"They'll never go for that"*
- *"We'll never be able to afford that"*
- *"That's not even realistic"*
- *"That's a really stupid idea"*
- *"Sure, and it'll eliminate someone's job"*
- *"And where will you get the money for it?"*
- *"You're kidding, right?"*

Each of these statements can be a significant hazard in the *Idea Garden.* They have the impact of toxic chemicals, drought, pests, floods, and temperature extremes. Remember that ideas are living things with the potential to give birth to other ideas—including your next idea.

Here are four ways to participate in the evolution of ideas.

- **Curiosity:** *"Tell me more about that idea"*
- **Concern:** *"Let's talk about how we can take care of some concerns I see with this"*
- **Interest:** *"That's a really different approach...let's see what we can do with it"*
- **Encouragement:** *"Let's do some research on that and check out what's actually possible rather than just guess or speculate about it"*

53 SUPPORT BUILDING

Howard Gardner, in his survey of creative giants like Picasso, Einstein, and Freud, tells us that all creative people have significant psychological and technical support preceding and during their most dramatic breakthroughs.

Inviting other people into the sketching, editing, improving, packaging, and selling phases of your creative process gives you potential you could never have on your own. From the quantum perspective, there is no greater myth than self-reliance.

54 THE "F" WORD

When your aim is to get support for your idea, persistence becomes more of a virtue than patience. For most of us, this requires a total reinventing of our (learned) concept of the "F" word—*failure*.

Failure comes in many forms. Ideas we can't use, research that leads us nowhere, experiments that give us more learning than results, ideas that don't win acceptance from the people with the bucks or the signatures. Failure is not a possibility in any creative process—it is an inevitability.

How do creative people look at and react to failure? Nobel Prize winner and holder of dozens of patents in biochemistry, Gertrude Elion, says that "Every failure is a step forward ... an opportunity to explore new things." This pretty much sums up her inventive spirit after decades of groundbreaking achievements.

Advertising award winner Leo Burnett puts it this way: "To swear off making mistakes is very easy. All you have to do is swear off having ideas."

In contrast to those of us who fall in love and hope to be faithful to our first and best ideas, we have the lessons of innovators. In the performing arts, choreographer extraordinaire, Twyla Tharp, looks at every idea and success (and failure) as a steppingstone to even better ones. Practicing idea detachment, she says that "The ultimate point of a piece for me is that it drives the next one. Does it open doors? That's the success of a piece."

From the world of car manufacturing, founder Soichiro Honda resonates: "Success represents the one percent of your work which results only from the ninety-nine percent that is called failure."

Our experience in school has apparently given us a very unrealistic view of failure as something to be avoided at all costs. For innovators, there is only one kind of failure: the failure to embrace failure as an infinite window into the soul of creative possibilities.

Anyone who practices idea evolution knows that, because creativity is a natural process, like any process in nature, there is no waste. "Bad" ideas lead to better ones. Things that don't work lead us to those that do. Waste is simply a total misunderstanding of creativity by people not trained in it.

55 NEVER SAY FAIL

1. In a survey of baseball greats, we find that the top 10 hitters took an average of 54 swings for each home run hit.

2. The Star Wars movie concept was rejected by 12 Hollywood studios before it was finally accepted.

3. The photocopying process was rejected as viable technology by IBM, GM and Dupont, among others.

4. Victor Kiam of Remington Razor fame rejected the $25,000 Velcro patent that has since led to over $6 Billion in sales.

5. Post It Notes failed in all four of its first market tests until creative ideas in marketing gave it one more lift to its multimillion dollar track record.

6. In the early 1980's an NBC executive was known to have said that there would be absolutely no future for any TV show featuring bars or multiple story lines.

7. In the 1950's, Sony's founder Aikio Morita tried unsuccessfully to market two products his engineers developed from American inventions, being told that there would never be a US market for either—the transistor radio and tape player.

8. In the 1962, Decca Records told the Beatles that groups with guitars were on their way "out".

9. In 1927 Warner Brothers president, Harry Warner, asked in a meeting one day: "Who wants to hear actors talk?"

10. The Swiss watchmakers, with over 80% of the watch market share worldwide, decided not to patent the quartz watch, believing no one would want such an "inferior" product.

The next time you run into or expect any resistance to your ideas, remember the words of Edison, originator of over 1000 patents: "I'll never say fail."

56 LEVERAGING RESISTANCE

People who resist new ideas typically bring to the innovation table important countersuggestions, questions, concerns, and secondary problems. If we listen and encourage their involvement, we not only have the chance to grow better ideas, we also win allies.

There is only one intelligent approach to anyone who is "negative" in a creative process: invite them to contribute everything they have, and more.

It's easy to become defensive about an idea, especially when people see it as fair game. It is equally challenging when your ideas lack support because of the politics at play.

Don't waste time trying to convert heretics and nonbelievers. Spend more time getting your best supporters involved in improving and selling your ideas. Politically effective people know from experience that fighting resistance sometimes strengthens it. It is smarter use of your time, resources, and connections to build a groundswell for your ideas that tips the balance of approval in your favor. It's smarter to build the minority you do have than to fight the majority you don't want to have.

57 FAIL FAST

If we have no choice about whether we'll encounter failure, we have two options: fail slow or fail fast. Innovation leaders choose the latter.

This translates into experimenting with ideas more often. Instead of talking or thinking or planning them on paper, take your ideas before they're fully formed and try them out in the field. The lessons you'll learn will give you not only quicker results, but better results.

An hour of experimenting and action learning is worth more than a hundred hours of polarizing speculation and debate. If you keep "getting more input" in order to prevent failure in innovation, forget it. You're going to have it no matter how many meetings you have. Do what the best do: *Fail fast.*

Ask any artist. Creativity is a always a commitment to experimentation. Some thinking can only be done by doing, not talking. Many organizations have found that they can develop new products in half the time and a quarter of the cost thanks to using first generation products as a test. The same can be said for first generation services.

As Tom Peters suggests: "The essence of successful innovation is, and always has been, constant experimentation."

58 EFFECTIVE PROPOSALS

When your group is ready to propose ideas to decision makers, here are a few features that increase your chances for winning support.

1. Buy-In

Buy-in comes from involvement. Remember, we support most what we help create. How have you involved decision makers at the beginning of your creativity process? Did you ask them to help you define requirements and parameters? Did you invite them to idea sessions, assign them to subgroups and make them feel welcome and valued for their ideas, concerns, and questions?

If you did, your proposal may be a ceremonial affirmation (translate: no brainer).

2. Multi-media

We all think in different languages. Finance people think in numbers, risk managers in risk-avoidance, engineers in pictures, operations in time and resource requirements. Translate any idea into the languages of those to whom you're proposing, and support will come your way. The more senses people use to experience your idea, the more chances you have to win their approval. Be creative.

3. Test Results

Nothing helps decision makers agree on an idea like results. If you have piloted your idea in the field and can present testimonials from pleased end-users and other critics, you have only made it more difficult for decision makers to ignore or neglect your idea. As Tom Peters reminds us, "Any new idea is, by definition, disruptive...building a groundswell through pilot projects in the field...simply turns out to be the most effective—and efficient—way to implement anything."

4. Choice Of Yesses

Master consultant, Alan Weiss CMC, includes in many of his proposals what he calls a "choice of yesses." Make it as easy for decision makers to say "yes" by never giving them only one option to accept or reject. Increase your chances for yes dramatically by always giving them several options to choose from. If you have invented different alternatives and variations, you're closer to yes than you think.

5. Divide & Conquer

Selling an idea to individuals in sometimes easier, for them and you, than to a group. There is less pressure for you to appeal to conflicting agendas at the same time, and less pressure for them to dance to the music of the politics at play. Before proposing ideas to a group, sell individual members first. Strategically target fence-sitters, silent supporters, and potential critical mass members. Then your group proposal becomes more likely to win support.

59 MAKING IDEAS MORE SELLABLE

1. Make it easier to operate or implement

2. Build in more esthetic or entertainment features

3. Think of how a group of artists might design or decorate it

4. Develop cheaper versions of it

5. Make it more portable

6. Make it more permanent

7. Get some high-profile or end-user endorsements for it

8. Make it safer, greener

9. Make it more challenging, dare-inviting

10. Build more functions into its features

11. Simplify or reduce its functions

12. Build in "attachments"

13. Appeal more to the "child" in its users

14. Make it more accessible

15. Offer more options

16. Design it with more do-it-yourself or self-serve functions

17. Design in more "done-for-you" options

18. Package it differently

19. Rename it

20. Propose a (no-charge) trial period

21. Design in "smart", automated & remote control features

This is just a short list to get your thinking started. The list is only limited to what your imagination allows. Be inventive!

Creative Organizations

60 Reinventing Organizations To Be More Inventive

An important opportunity for collaborative creativity today is the design of organizations. Reinventing the organization means reinventing the way tasks are assigned, processes are structured, and the way teams are developed and used. Organizations can be designed to inhibit or to unleash people's collective potentials for creativity.

The evolution toward more collaborative creativity is ultimately a self-reinforcing process. As the organization better supports collaborative creativity, people and teams become more creative and collaborative. Their creativity together inevitably touches every organizational system, structure, practice, and relationship. This leads to a more innovative organization, leading to more innovative people and a pattern that only repeats itself in a thousand fractal ways.

1996 marked Sears' return to its performance potentials with macro- and micro-level changes in how it nurtures and leverages its employees' information and ideas for a more competitive mix of products and services. That's the inventive spirit—truly satisfied only when experimenting.

Everything is up for grabs. Sacred cows are finding themselves the hit of reorganization barbecues in more than a few organizations across fields and industries. Health care, manufacturing, education, government, retail, and engineering and construction firms are all feeling the shift. We are cooking up new paradigms.

Reorganizing for creativity can start anywhere and work its way through the organization. It can start right where you are. You have the power to question practices and policies that stifle collaborative creativity. More importantly, you have the power to suggest ways to reinvent processes and projects so that people can take more innovative initiative than ever before.

61 CREATIVITY CULTURES

Annabile reports on a study of 165 R&D scientists over a large cross-section of organizations. The study focuses on organizational variables that support creativity, invention, and innovation. The top 5 include:

1. *Freedom over work*

Nothing unleashes new ideas like having the freedom to make decisions in your work. Empowered teams have a far greater capacity for innovation than teams who have managers, for whom job security is to control people's work (and thinking) for them.

2. *Encouragement for original thinking*

In creative organizations, ideas that initially "make no sense" are treated with at least as much respect as those that do. Originality is valued because the organization strives to succeed by differentiating its value from other suppliers.

3. *Boundarylessness*

A leader in our thinking about boundarylessness is GE's Jack Welch. According to Jack, "What we value most is boundarylessness...when there are no limits to whom you'll see, where you'll go, what you touch, the results are remarkable." GE has certainly seen a lion's share of results since it began practicing boundarylessness.

4. Challenging, time-urgent projects

We recall award-winning artist Charlotte Lees, saying that the more restrictions she has, the more creative she is. Anyone who works with challenging projects on a daily basis knows first hand their potential for stimulating creativity.

5. Time for research

According to cybernetics innovator and anthropologist, Gregory Bateson, organizations are conscious entities that generate, process, and produce information. The same could be said about any project or problem-solving team. Margaret Wheatley explains that teams work because they "Generate the very energy that orders the universe—information." Time spent in research is time getting more in touch with the very essence of life that inspires all things inventive.

62 ORGANIZATIONAL HAZARDS IN THE IDEA GARDEN

We have a moral obligation to protect ideas, especially in their initial, fragile states. Organizational design and culture has a huge impact on the fate of fragile ideas that have the potential to lead us toward breakthrough results.

All organizations have a wide range of hazards that are harmful to living ideas.

- Idea Bottlenecks

The chain of command design requires that ideas pass through several people who are busy just trying to keep up with their to-do lists. Each link in the chain becomes a potential bottleneck where living ideas can get stuck and suffocate from lack of fresh dialogue and exposure to information and other ideas. When bottlenecks are eliminated, information, and ideas flow freely.

- Quality Slogans

As slogans, "Do it right the first time" and "Strive for zero variation" are not the messages you want to send teams who need to be more inventive and reinventive. The creative process guarantees "right" only the second or fortieth time. We all need to be thankful that Thomas Edison was more than willing to doing it "wrong" over 1700 times before he gave us the light bulb. Variation, too, is a goal in the creative process—in the world of ideas more variety leads to better. Not all failure and variation is bad. When creativity is supported like crazy, it can and will lead to things done right the first time and zero negative variation.

- Short Ends Of The Carrot

Nothing destroys the creative spirit like emphasizing extrinsic incentives that leave those most proud of their ideas feeling less valued because they received only a fraction of what "big idea" people get. If your organization is at all serious about creativity and innovation, it needs to encourage ideas that are so rich in their evolution that they cannot be traced back to any individual "ownership." Don't destroy the natural, intrinsic value of the collaborative process in creativity by instituting a piecework approach.

- "Team Player" Guilt

Watch out for how people use the word "teamwork." Don't let it become an excuse for pressuring people to conform to the group's majority voices. "Come on, you're not being a team player" only prevents value-added alternatives, questions, and considerations that can only make existing ideas better. Redefine "team player" as someone willing to present differences that add potential value to a collaborative process.

- Idea Stealers

In a manufacturing plant, employees are asked for ideas when problems occur on the lines. Managers and engineers working on the problem will take these ideas and claim credit for them whether they are presented in their original form or enhanced by improvements. Try to get most line people in this plant today to give up any ideas, much less spend time with creative opportunities while chatting at lunch or walking the dog. Do whatever you can to get credit (the more public the better) to everyone and anyone who contributed even the least to an idea.

- Rewarding Conformity

In many organizations, conformity to policy and procedure is a virtue. It leads to favorable reviews and promotions. Conformity is the opposite to creativity. Creativity blooms where it is measured, promoted, and encouraged through words and actions.

- No Time "Away From Work"

Managers preach continuous improvement in one meeting, then in the next refer to the time people spend in collaborative creativity as time "away from work." In innovative organizations, nothing matters more than ideas. Ideas are the work. Results are simply the logical manifestations of the quality of the ideas we cultivate together. Aside from that, creativity is not a matter of time. An inspired spark of an idea can occur instantly.

- Job Descriptions

Job descriptions were invented primarily in situations where communication was at its worst. They divide up all predictable tasks among those available for assignments. This creates an ugly phenomenon called "my job." We can accurately credit job descriptions with those famous words "It's not my job." We can design work in ways that prevent duplication and gaps and still get everyone being collaborative in their creative processes.

If you have any opportunity to reduce or eliminate these hazards in your organization, get started yesterday. If you don't have the "power" to impact them, take and make opportunities to suggest ideas aimed at preventing and reducing them.

63 PATRIARCHY & CREATIVITY

A patriarchy is a system which divides people into two classes of power, information, responsibility, and reward haves and have-nots. Traditional organizations are patriarchies by design or by practice. Managers are in the class of haves and employees are in the class of have-nots. Boundaries exist everywhere—vertically and horizontally, internally and externally.

Creative people are a species at risk in a patriarchal environment. Every boundary is a barrier to the flow of ideas and the empowerment of their parents.

Only when people share in information and power, do they have the ability to develop ideas into practical, realistic, unique solutions for themselves, their customers and their markets. Only when people share in responsibility and rewards do they feel compelled to take the risks required in any creative process.

64 THE POWER OF PARTNERSHIPS

Celebrated biologist and writer Lewis Thomas suggests that when we form partnerships, we are participating in process as old as nature itself. He says, "The urge to form partnerships, to link up in collaborative arrangements, is perhaps the oldest, strongest, and most fundamental force in nature."

Best-selling author and consultant Peter Block contrasts partnership with patriarchal models of organizational design. According to Peter, "Partnership means to be connected to another in a way that the power between us is roughly balanced." In a patriarchy, the tradition in most organizations, we are divided into two classes of power haves and have-not's. In a partnership, the gap is closed through education, empowerment, and equity.

There are four core requirements for partnerships.

1. Shared responsibilities

In a partnership, everyone on a team—whether we're talking about a project, function or organizational team—shares accountability for decisions, outcomes, and innovations (changes). No one in a process is more responsible; suppliers are not more responsible than customers for quality. In this paradigm that goes well beyond "customer is king/queen", responsibility is shared. It is after all a partnership, not a patriarchy. No one is responsible for anyone else's performance, success, satisfaction or development. Everyone shares it.

2. Shared resources

Everyone shares information, materials, technology, facilities, expert information, and opportunities. Resources are optimized because we plan together their purchase, development, and use. The partnership world is not competitively divided into winners with more and losers with less. From the quantum perspective, when one part of a system wins, everyone wins.

3. Shared rights

Everyone shares a fundamental freedom to agree or disagree, say yes or no. This is a dramatic and profound contrast to parental patriarchy only the privileged (managers) are given the right to say yes or no. In a patriarchy, a manager is there to be served and can say no to the request of an employee who does not share this freedom. In a partnership, the preferred mode of influence is dialogue, since rights of agreement are shared. Partnership means decision by consensus, not coercion.

4. Shared risks

Everyone shares the gains and losses that result from collaborative efforts, outcomes, and decisions. One of the hallmarks of patriarchal organizations is the implicit contract between child-employee and parent-manager to trade loyalty for protection. In a partnership no such trade is acceptable. Our paychecks and security mutually reflect our collective successes and setbacks. As Peter Block says, the only guarantee in a partnership is that it will be an adventure. Not your cup of espresso? Find, buy, or build a nice patriarchy for yourself.

65 PARTNERSHIP OPPORTUNITIES

Opportunities to develop partnerships are limited only to our collective imaginations. Here are four examples.

1. Employee-manager partnerships

Managers become suppliers of information, expert knowledge, resources, coaching, and facilitation services to self-directed teams of employees. Together they share opportunities and accountabilities, power, and rewards.

2. Customer-supplier partnerships

Organizations are living systems of internal and external customer and supplier relationships. As partnerships, they solve each other's problems together. Out of deep appreciation for their interdependency, they treat each other's success as their own. Team up to solve each other's problems and mutually gain from common opportunities.

3. Benchmarking partnerships

Organizations sharing benchmarking experience work as partners to import and export each other's learning. They become stronger and more innovative together than they ever could be apart.

4. Strategic alliance partnerships

Competitive and noncompetitive organizations team up for strategic projects aimed at standard-setting, collaborative research and development, and resource-sharing.

Partnerships work. They bring about the sharing of responsibilities, resources, rights, and risks in a way that unleashes creative opportunities and potentials.

Partnership organizations give employees a liberating and profound sense of control over their work. This is no small advantage for companies looking for sustainable approaches to employee satisfaction. Most importantly, "Creativity will flourish when employees feel a sense of control over their own work", says Monsongo Moukwa. It has worked for artists and inventors for a long time—why not with employees and managers?

The Tofflers, looking at the requirements of the organization of the future agrees. "Companies are hurrying to empower employees...(and to) push as many decisions down from the top out to the periphery." Creativity thrives at the edge of chaos.

66 WHAT ABOUT CONTROL IN CREATIVE ORGANIZATIONS?

Control and consistency have always been priorities in (patriarchal) organizations. Creativity brings to organizations a different kind of control. It is not the control of machines, but the control of living things—two completely different sets of dynamics at work.

Peter Block on traditional approaches to control in organizations: "Strategies of control and consistency, for all their strengths tend to be expensive, are slow to react to the marketplace, and drain passion from human beings."

Control and consistency are only virtues when the goal to keep things the same—to keep them from being any different tomorrow than they are today. This is hardly desirable in a world where new and different outperforms old and same.

Margaret Wheatley, talking about organizational design from a quantum perspective, says that "In life, the issue is not control, but dynamic relatedness." Diana Zohar speaking directly about the quantum perspective that underlines the whole spirit of partnerships tells us that, in quantum systems (like organizations), the more elements are fixed, the less they function together as a whole.

Collaborative creativity replaces control with dialogue—the essence of partnership. In a world where we are given the choices of creativity or control, successful artists and inventors who transform the way we look at the world and live in it choose creativity every time.

67 CARROT CAKE ANYONE?

Breakthroughs! author points out that "Incentives aren't the reason 3M gets creativity" from its Post It Note inventors, Silver and Fry. In a series of conversations, Inventor Hall Of Fame inductees make it clear that carrots—the promise of prizes and promotions and industry fame—did not get them up in the morning. According to most of these inventors, they often worked in environments that were somewhere between apathetic, cynical, and resistant to their efforts.

Curiosity has always been the driving force behind their passion to invent and reinvent their world. Hard to believe that something as overlooked as curiosity could be that powerful, but it is.

Alfie Kohn, talking about hundreds of research studies on external incentives, says that groups competing for prizes tend to demonstrate lower quality, lower risk taking, and lower creativity. This makes sense when you realize how interconnected these three phenomena are. Sure, this is counterintuitive to common beliefs. But then as Buddhist teacher Robert Thurman likes to say, truth always contains paradox and contradiction.

68 THE ROLE OF LEADERS IN THE CREATIVE ORGANIZATION

Things do not work simply because all of the right pieces have been assembled in the same space. Your car as parts in a large box in your driveway will do nothing car-like for you or anyone. Things work only to the degree that all the pieces are connected correctly and continuously.

The role of leader in the creative organization is to connect people in an environment of boundaryless exploration, invention, and reinvention. Creativity-promoting leaders spend a lot of time and energy introducing people who don't know each other, calling meetings between people who don't work together, sharing decision making with people who have never made decisions together, telling success stories about ideas to people who are clueless about the creative potentials of their own environment. These leaders go out of their way to open the books of the business and educate people in how to read, understand and use them.

This is one way to look at the role of leader. General Electric's CEO Jack Welch gives us a simpler version: "My job is to listen, search for, think of and spread ideas."

Any questions?

69 HAVE FUN, MAKE MONEY

Browse through a few vision and mission statements today. If your organization has them, look at them. Why do so many vision and mission statements go on and on about what essentially comes down to two things—*having fun and making money*. All those extra words tease us into believing there is more to creating and serving markets. There isn't.

Creativity plays a direct role in both strategic objectives. Nothing is less fun than work that does not demand or include creativity, invention, and innovation. There is perhaps nothing more satisfying (can we say, even fun) than work that continuously requires collaborative use of our imaginations in the service of new and useful ways to make things faster, better, cheaper, and easier.

Nothing makes money today more than products and services that are new and improved. Both are driven by collaborative creativity. It takes new ideas to get to new levels of performance. It takes new ideas to solve problems that keep work from being fun and money-making for everyone in the partnership. Improvement is continuous when creativity is continuous.

70 FUN

Maybe it's the Puritan influence in our culture. We have somehow linked seriousness with problem-solving and work. There is however, not a lot of documented evidence that seriousness adds value to the creative process. The evidence has been that a spirit of playfulness only adds value to the process and outcomes of problem solving in partnerships. If anything, an inflexible commitment to seriousness maintains the ruts of thinking that limit fresh possibilities. There are more than a few ways to breathe life into the organization. Unfortunately, some of these might temporarily cause some serious people to get even more serious for a while, but give it time. They'll come around.

- The next time you're tempted to torture people with another "time management" seminar, cut the time it half and spend the other half inviting someone to come in and talk about humor.

- Inventory your training library. Are you missing tapes of Lilly Tomlin or George Carlin live? What about old Laurel & Hardy flicks? Get busy tending the other side of your library garden of inspiring resources.

- Feed the cartoon mill with any (nonoffensive, of course) material—there is plenty of it, starting with newspaper and New Yorker cartoons. Make a rule that everyone must bring a cartoon to share in your next staff or regional meeting.

- Work with the group from that confuses idea sessions with skeet shooting contests. Issue waterguns and introduce the rule: Get anyone caught shooting down someone's idea. Watch people walk out of meetings just a little dryer every week.

- Expand the "Casual Friday" concept to include "theme" Fridays—Western Dress Fridays, Formal Eveningwear Fridays, Sports Gear Fridays, Blue-Only (any color) Fridays. Business Futurist Roger Herman CMC, author of *Keeping Good People* suggests dressing creatively any day—within reason.

- Install toys. Install a box of Toobers & Zots, tinkertoys and clay on conference room tables. Encourage play before, during and after meetings. Have prize-free contests (just for fun...imagine) for the most imaginative displays of ideas. One innovative facilitator, Joyce Gioia CMC, gives small prizes to participants in her seminars.

- Set parts of new employee orientations to music and have managers participate. Move orientations to parks, rented museum conference rooms, art studios, and anywhere that might send interesting and important messages about what the organization values. Or do it just because it might be more fun.

- Instead of dreadfully dry, one-dimensional paper and pencil surveys of customers or employees, collect information with hand-held videos. Let them have the quality of wedding videos where people are asked to offer a minute of congratulations. In this case, it's feedback, suggestions, and input. Five minutes of these can often be worth more than twenty pages of lifeless tables and charts.

Be imaginative. Look around the organization for ways to liven things up. The possibilities are endless. In the words of Aristotle, "Pleasure in the job puts perfection in the work."

Here's the physics and politics of fun. Fun is more interesting. Interesting makes the organization a better supplier, customer, and employer. What else do you have on your list of strategic objectives?

71 BOTTOM LINE

People will be and can be creative together in any kind of environment. The potentials are greater however, in an environment that treats ideas as the most important natural resource on the planet.

Do whatever you can to invite the continuous reinvention of your environment to reflect this priority. Build an environment where it is easy for people to be open-minded, inventive, provocative, and practical. Refuse to work on ideas in isolation. Refuse to treat any problem as unsolvable or impossible. Work hard and smart to eliminate barriers to continuous creativity across boundaries inside and outside your organization.

In a retrospective on what we as a planet have done in the last 150 years, it is clear that we've already done (what was once deemed by experts as) "the impossible." We've been there, done it, and bought the T-shirt. As long as we share the opportunities, we can easily continue this legacy.

72 TOP LINE

Every bottom line of value begins with the top line—the line of vision. Collaborative creativity is a vision to strive for. Every time your organization reaches new heights in productivity or profitability, it does so thanks to ideas. Make creativity together your top line of vision, and the bottom lines will reflect it. Unleash the power of minds sharing the space of information and imagination. On an individual, team, and organizational level, what we call "reality" is nothing less than an infinite field of potentiality.

In the words of philosopher Miguel de Unamuno: "All we are given is possibilities."

Sources

Experts in design tell us that inspiration is a matter of exposure to a variety of elements that together go into creating a unique event or product. Each of the 72 essays were inspired and informed by a variety of sources. This reference list can be useful for continuing learning in the areas of collaboration and creativity.

1 Chopra, Deepak. *Quantum Healing.* Bantam Books, 1989.
2 Nayak, P. Ranganath & Ketteringham, John M. *Breakthroughs!* Rawson Associates, 1986.
3 Higgins, James. *Innovate or Evaporate.* The New Management Publishing Company, 1995.
4 Toffler, Alvin & Heidi. *Creating a New Civilization.* Turner Publishing, 1994.
5 Carey, Steven. *Steven Carey's Invention Book.* Workman, 1985.
6 Weisberg, Robert. *Creativity.* W.H. Freeman, 1995.
    Halem, Henry. Interview, Summer 1996.
    Picariello, Martha L., Amabile, Teresa M. & Grykiewicz, Stanley S. *The Motivations, Cognitive Style, and Work Environments of Successful Inventors.* Inventure Place, 1995.
7 Gardner, Howard. *Creating Minds.* Basic Books, 1993.
8 Nayak, P. Ranganath & Ketteringham, John M. *Breakthroughs!* Rawson Associates, 1986.
9 de Bono, Edward. *Serious Creativity.* The McQuaig Group, 1992.
10 Augros, Robert & Stanciu, George. *The New Biology.* Shambhala, 1987.
    Nayak, P. Ranganath & Ketteringham, John M. *Breakthroughs!* Rawson Associates, 1986.
11 Bogan, Christopher E. *Benchmarking for Best Practices.* McGraw-Hill, 1994.
12 Chopra, Deepak. *Escaping the Prison of the Intellect.* Sound Recording. New World Library, 1992.
13 de Bono, Edward. *Serious Creativity.* The McQuaig Group, 1992.
    Higgins, James. *Innovate or Evaporate.* The New Management Publishing Company, 1995
14 de Bono, Edward. *Serious Creativity.* The McQuaig Group, 1992.
15 Weisberg, Robert. *Creativity.* W.H. Freeman, 1995
    Logsdon, Tom. *Breaking Through.* Addison-Wesley, 1993.
    Moje, Claus. Interview, Summer 1995.

Thompson, Charles "Chic". *What a Great Idea!* HarperPerennial, 1992.

Lees, Charlotte. Interview, Winter 1995.

16 de Bono, Edward. *The Greatest Thinkers*. Putnam, 1976.

Barker, Joel. Quoted in Interview Week, 5/18/92.

Gardner, Howard. *Creating Minds*. Basic Books, 1993.

Young, Brent. Cleveland Museum of Art Gallery Talk, May 1994

Sternberg, Robert J. *Defying the Crowd*. Free Press, 1995.

17 Suzuki, Shunryu. *Zen Mind, Beginner's Mind*. John Weatherhill, 1970.

18 de Bono, Edward. *Sur/petition*. Harper Business, 1992.

19 Talbot, Michael. *Beyond the Quantum*. McMillan, 1986.

Chopra, Deepak. *Quantum Healing*. Bantam Books, 1989.

de Bono, Edward. *Serious Creativity*. The McQuaig Group, 1992.

Aguayo, Rafael. *Dr. Deming*. Lyle Stuart, 1990.

20 Weisberg, Robert. *Creativity*. W.H. Freeman, 1995.

21 Chopra, Deepak. *Escaping the Prison of the Intellect*. Sound Recording. New World Library, 1992.

22 de Bono, Edward. *Serious Creativity*. The McQuaig Group, 1992.

23 Zohar, Dianna & Marshall, Ian. *The Quantum Society*. Morrow, 1994

Wheatley, Margaret. Interview. Industry Week, 4/18/95.

Henry, Jane (Ed.). *Creative Management*. Sage, 1991.

24 Augros, Robert & Stanciu, George. The New Biology. Shambhala, 1987.

25 Ray, Michael & Rinzler, Alan. *New Paradigms in Business*. Bantam Books, 1987.

Kohn, Alfie. *No Contest*. Houghton Mifflin, 1986.

Inc 1/93

26 Weisberg, Robert. *Creativity*. W.H. Freeman, 1995

Logsdon, Tom. *Breaking Through*. Addison-Wesley, 1993.

27 Peters, Tom. The Pursuit of WOW. Vintage Books, 1994.

28 Kohn, Alfie. *No Contest*. Houghton Mifflin, 1986.

Moukwa, Mosongo. *Journal of Creative Behavior*, 1st Quarter 1995.

Picariello, Martha L., Amabile, Teresa M. & Grykiewicz,Stanley S. *The Motivations, Cognitive Style, and Work Environments of Successful Inventors.*Inventure Place, 1995.

Cleveland Plain Dealer, 4/22/94

Ray, Michael & Rinzler, Alan. *New Paradigms in Business*. Bantam Books, 1987.

Hall, Doug. *Jump Start Your Brain*. Warner Books, 1995.

Jackson, Phil. Interview. Tricycle, Summer 1994.

29 Bohm, David. *Thought as a System*. Routledge, 1992.

30 Burrus, Dan. *Technotrends.* Harper Business, 1993.
Diaz, Adriana. Freeing the Creative Spirit. HarperCollins, 1992.
Yenne, Bill. *100 Inventions that Shaped World History.* Bluewood Books, 1993.
31 Schrage, Michael. *No More Teams.* Currency Doubleday, 1989.
32 Ryan, Kathleen & Oestreich. *Driving Fear out of the Workplace.* Jossey-Bass, 1991.
33 Schrage, Michael. *No More Teams.* Currency Doubleday, 1989.
34 Ray, Michael. *Creativity In Business.* Doubleday, 1986.
Logsdon, Tom. *Breaking Through.* Addison-Wesley, 1993
Robbins, Anthony. *Awaken the Giant Within.* Simon & Schuster Trade, 1992.
Noone. Donald J. *Creative Problem Solving.* Barron's 1993.
35 de Bono, Edward. *Lateral Thinking.* Harper & Row, 1970.
39 de Bono, Edward. *Serious Creativity.* The McQuaig Group, 1992.
40 Grossman, Stephen. *Journal of Creative Behavior.* 1995.
41 Inc Magazine, January 1993.
42 Schrage, Michael. *No More Teams.* Currency Doubleday, 1989.
43 Inc Magazine, 1/93
44 Schrage, Michael. *No More Teams.* Currency Doubleday, 1989.
45 Schrage, Michael. *No More Teams.* Currency Doubleday, 1989.
46 Ryan, Kathleen & Oestreich. *Driving Fear out of the Workplace.* Jossey-Bass, 1991.
47 Stacey, Ralph D. *Managing the Unknowable.* Jossey-Bass, 1992
Levin, Rob. Interview, Summer 1996.
48 *Creativity Infusion.* Harper & Row, 1989.
50 Ryan, Kathleen & Oestreich. *Driving Fear out of the Workplace.* Jossey-Bass, 1991.
51 Wheatley, Margaret. *Leadership and the New Science.* Berrett-Koehler, 1992.
52 de Bono, Edward. *Serious Creativity.* The McQuaig Group, 1992.
53 Gardner, Howard. *Creating Minds.* Basic Books, 1993.
54 Inventure Place Exhibit, Akron OH.
New York Times, 4/11/95.
New York Times, 4/30/95.
55 Higgins, James. *Innovate or Evaporate.* The New Management Publishing Company, 1995.
New York Times Magazine, 5/14/95.
56 Peters, Tom. *Thriving on Chaos.* Alfred A. Knopf, 1987.
57 Peters, Tom. *The Pursuit of WOW.* Vintage Books, 1994.
58 Talk to Institute Of Management Consultants, Spring 1995.
59 Lees, Charlotte. Interview, Winter 1995.
60 Higgins, James. *Innovate or Evaporate.* The New Management Publishing Company, 1995.

61 Sternberg, Robert J. *Defying the Crowd.* Free Press, 1995.
    Fortune, 12/13/93.
    Bateson, Gregory. *Mind and Nature.* Dutton, 1978.
    Wheatley, Margaret. *Leadership and the New Science.* Berrett-Koehler, 1992.
62 Higgins, James. *Innovate or Evaporate.* The New Management Publishing Company, 1995.
63 Block, Peter. *Stewardship.* Berrett-Koehler, 1993.
64 Block, Peter. *Stewardship.* Berrett-Koehler, 1993.
    Thomas, Lewis. *The Lives of a Cell.* Bantam Books, 1974.
65 Block, Peter. *Stewardship.* Berrett-Koehler, 1993.
66 Toffler, Alvin & Heidi. *Creating a New Civilization.* Turner Publishing, 1994. Berrett-Koehler, 1992.
    Zohar, Dianna & Marshall, Ian. *The Quantum Society.* Morrow, 1994.
67 Inventure Place Conference, July 1995.
68 Fortune 12/13/93.
69 Hall, Doug. *Jump Start Your Brain.* Warner Books, 1995
70 Herman, Roger & Gioia, Joyce. Interviews, May 1996.
71 Inventure Place Conference, July 1995.
72 Chopra, Deepak. *Quantum Healing.* Bantam Books, 1989.
    New York Times, 7/21/95.

Contacting the Author

Jack Ricchiuto may be contacted for inquiries, speaking engagements and interviews at the following places:

on the Internet, ricchiuto@msn.com

by phone at (216) 766-8280

by fax at (216) 651-4565

or by mail at

> The Ricchiuto Group
> 3020 Carroll Avenue
> Cleveland, Ohio 44113

Order Information

Orders for *Collaborative Creativity* and all other **Oakhill Press** titles can be placed by phone at (800) 322-6657, by fax at (330) 836-3311, by e-mail via orders@oakhillpress.com, or by mail at

> Oakhill Press
> PO BOX 5351
> Akron, Ohio 44334-0351

● check out our web site at www.oakhillpress.com ●

8/6/99 Kid & Families

According to Piaget - between ages 7 + 10 (dif
ch love to make up rules for their games.
For example "you have to go back to the
green bucket & hit the (paddle) ball."
A ~~bonus~~ Dad or Mom playing w/ them can
plug into the approach — & also use it
inform & get things done.